JOHN MATTHEWS
and CHARLES NEWINGTON

the FOOL'S
NEW JOURNEY
TAROT

Sixty Triumphs for a New Dawn

REDFeather™

MIND | BODY | SPIRIT

4880 Lower Valley Road, Atglen, PA 19310

Designed by BMac
Type set in Minion/New Frank

ISBN: 978-0-7643-6768-7
Printed in China

Published by REDFeather Mind, Body, Spirit
An imprint of Schiffer Publishing, Ltd.
4880 Lower Valley Road
Atglen, PA 19310
Phone: (610) 593-1777; Fax: (610) 593-2002
Email: Info@redfeathermbs.com
Web: www.redfeathermbs.com

For our complete selection of fine books on this and related subjects,
please visit our website at www.redfeathermbs.com. You may also write
for a free catalog.

The Fool represents the soul of everyman, which, after it is clothed in a body, appears on earth and goes through the life experiences depicted in the 21 cards of the Major Arcana, sometimes thought of as archetypes of the subconscious. Let each reader use his imagination and find here his own map of the soul's quest, for these are symbols that are deep within each one of us.

—Eden Gray, *The Complete Guide to the Tarot*

CONTENTS

FOREWORD

by ANDREA ASTE

Considerate la vostra semenza:
fatti non foste a viver come bruti,
ma per seguir virtute e canoscenza

Consider your origin;
you were not born to live like brutes,
but to follow virtue and knowledge.

—Dante, *Divina Commedia*, Inferno, canto XXVI, 118

It was a gloomy day. Dark the sky, dark the earth. That kind of darkness that slowly penetrates into your soul and smothers it. In the realm of Death, every day was the same. But that day, something unpredictable happened. Something fought against that ominous darkness. A light was made, and immediately it shone brighter and brighter. A little man lit it. His name was Primo Levi. He did not know it, but with his simple gesture he would change everything, for himself as well as for everyone else. That day, in the cold winter of 1944, in the unspeakable horror of Auschwitz, he did the unthinkable; he started to recite Dante's *Commedia* for himself and his inmates, almost whispering it, in secret, for fear to be caught by the guards. Telling the story of Dante's imaginary journey from Hell to Heaven, he gave them hope, he saved them, and with them he saved himself. Day after day, they navigated the *Divine Comedy*. The light became inextinguishable. Years later, Levi would become a famous writer, his books translated into every language. He shared that light with everyone. Among all the canti of the *Commedia* he was reciting, he kept coming back to one in particular: canto XXVI, which recounts Dante's meeting with Odysseus and his last voyage from Ithaca to the end of the world. A journey within a journey. . . . Maybe this is one of the reasons why Levi, out of all the inspiring books ever written, chose Dante. The journey! Something marvellous happens when we go out (or are forced out) of our comfort zone and embark in a new adventure; we accept life in its totality, in its depth and mystery. We become fully alive! Journeys give us new challenges, new rewards, a purpose, and, above all, the opportunity to grow, to be better human beings. As one of my favourite poets, Edgar Lee Master, wrote:

For love was offered me and I shrank from its disillusionment;
Sorrow knocked at my door, but I was afraid;
Ambition called to me, but I dreaded the chances.
Yet all the while I hungered for meaning in my life.
And now I know that we must lift the sail
And catch the winds of destiny
Wherever they drive the boat.

—George Gray, *Spoon River Anthology*

The journey is the most enthralling metaphor of life; one to which we have returned for millennia. From the beginning of humankind, we have defined ourselves, as humans, as being on a journey. And, indeed, we are on a constant quest, always looking for something outside ourself, be it an answer, knowledge, fulfillment, love. . . . It is not surprising that our first myths and storytelling were narratives of incredible journeys: *The Epic of Gilgamesh*, the Mayan *Popol Vuh*, *The Odyssey*, *The Tale of Princess Kaguya*, *A True Story* (Ἀληθῆ διηγήματα - Alēthē diēgēmata) by Lucian of Samosata. . . .

It does not even matter if the voyage is real or fantastic, because, from the imaginary adventures of *The Little Prince* to the diaries of British explorer Freya Stark, there is an identical *fil rouge*; in order to grow and know ourselves, we have to confront the "Other"; namely, "everything that is not us"; in other words, we have to accept the challenges that Destiny offers us, discovering and testing the limits of our individuality. If Joseph Campbell's theory is correct, every story is a journey, or better, a hero's journey. . . . There is no escape! Whatever interpretation we give (psychological, metaphorical, sociological, etc.) to this omnipresent concept, we are defined by it. And Tarot is not an exception! We can interpret the sequence of arcana as the Fool's Journey, and it is, indeed, an incredibly interesting and powerful way of analysing the cards. But, now, something even more stimulating is happening: the Fool is on a new journey! John Matthews's idea to reinvent Tarot is, to put the matter in simple terms, sublime. Many artists and authors have been redesigning Tarot, giving it new forms, shapes, meanings . . . but what John has done here has the depth of a beautifully refined intellectual game; the new sequence is deep and rich in meaning. Nothing is here by mere chance. Everything is carefully studied and yet natural, spontaneous. The new sequence flows like a river carrying you to the depth of an amazing cobalt sea. Chaos, History, The Observer, Healing, and Eternity are a few of the many new concepts and new challenges that await for The Fool (and for us) to be discovered. *The Fool's New Journey Tarot* captures the reader's imagination with the beauty of its meanings as well as the elegance of Charles Newington's style. The minimalism of the shapes and the purity of the colours used are powerful because immediate and suggestive, and yet, every time one gazes at a card, they will see something new, they will have different feelings and intuitions. Like a mirror reflecting in a mirror, there is no end of how far you can go, or how deep. . . . in this deck, infinity is looking back at you, with its marvels.

I was mesmerized by *The Fool's New Journey Tarot* from the first time John sent me the early cards, and, then, when I received what I cannot define with other words than The Epic of The New Fool's Journey, I was totally captured! I was unable to turn my attention to other directions for days. Fragments of poetry and images kept popping into my mind. A strange and marvellous experience! John has written a fascinating visionary and inspiring adventure. I think he has not only reinvented Tarot, but given it an epic dimension, with the depth and beauty of poetry. John has honoured Tarot as few have ever managed to do. A light is lit, once again. . . .

London, November 2022

INTRODUCTION

THE CREATION OF *THE FOOL'S NEW JOURNEY TAROT*

It was during the first lockdown of 2020, during the worldwide coronavirus pandemic, that I began to think of *The Fool's New Journey Tarot*. The world had grown silent, but work was still coming in and I was creating what would become *The Goblin Market Tarot* (Watkins, 2021). Then, as I sat in the garden thinking about the way I would shape the traditional meanings of the cards to fit a 19th-century poem, I suddenly found myself asking this: Are the archetypes of the Tarot set in stone? Not the images so much—these are fluid enough to generate countless new versions every year—but the basic meanings and applications.

I knew, of course, that despite various claims to trace the origins back to Egypt and beyond, the Tarot is a more recent phenomenon—certainly in the form we know it today. Tarot emerged in the 15th century from ordinary card decks, while the 22 Trumps or Triumphs derived from allegorical processional displays beloved of the Italian city states. Over the next 300 years it evolved as a game, *Tarocchi,* played initially in Italy and soon spreading to France and Germany and thereafter throughout most of Europe. The more esoteric use of the cards as a magical device for answering questions regarding the daily mysteries of life is no older than the late 18th century, while its truly occult focus came to the fore only in the mid-1800s.

In all this time, the decks have remained largely unchanged. In Italy during the 15th century, regional variations abounded, some with more, some with fewer cards. These were added to include other ideas and characters: famous soldiers, gods and goddesses, philosophers and kings. In one instance, the 16th-century *Minchiate Tarot*, trumps were added, representing the elements, the ideas of Faith, Hope, and Charity, and zodiacal signs, taking it to 96 cards. The pip cards, lacking detailed imagery, emerged from the original cartomantic usage and were based, with additions, on the four playing-card suits. Other than this, very little changed. In our own age, a vast variety of Tarots covering just about every aspect of life and endeavour have appeared—but in most cases these have stuck to the basic pattern: 22 majors and 56 minors (themselves bearing meanings derived from the 19th century). Even the order of the triumphs has not always kept to the same order—though the titles of the cards have hardly changed, beyond *The Papesse* (female pope) becoming *The High Priestess* and *The Pope* becoming *The Hierophant* in more modern times.

Then, in the 18th century, a group of people, including Court de Gebelin (1725–1784) and Paul Christian, the pseudonym of Jean-Baptiste Pitois (1811–1887), started to develop the traditional card decks by adding their own (mostly esoteric) understanding of what these meant. In the 19th century, ritual magicians such as A. E. Waite (1857–1942) and Aleister Crowley (1875–1947) took this further, looking back to the times before Tarocci was created, and adding layers of meaning to each card. The previous "pip" cards, which showed multiples of coins, swords, cups, and wands (each with its own history), began to be replaced by detailed images that told the story hidden in the card. In our own time, these have become so fixed in our consciousness—along with the pictorial images produced by Pamela Coleman Smith and Lady Frieda Harris—that it seemed they were going to remain that way forever. However, one development struck a chord in me from the start. This was included in the work of Eden Gray in the 1960s, and in particular her *Complete Guide to the Tarot* (1970), in which she proposed the idea of the Fool's Journey, linking everything to a single passage from ignorance to knowing. Her statement of this, which I have placed at the head of this book, still describes this as clearly as anyone can:

The Fool represents the soul of everyman, which, after it is clothed in a body, appears on earth and goes through the life experiences depicted in the 21 cards of the Major Arcana, sometimes thought of as archetypes of the subconscious. Let each reader use his imagination and find here his own map of the soul's quest, for these are symbols that are deep within each one of us.

On that particular day, as clouds crossed the sky and light and shadows played across the lawn in our garden, I found myself asking: Who said we had to have the same meanings—with a few minor details—for every Tarot deck produced? I had myself devised over 13 of these, and now I felt that something new was required—something that would bring Tarot into the present with ideas and concepts of which the originators of the first 15th-century decks either had little or no understanding or did not possess the language to explain.

Nor was it simply a matter of updating the images to show people in modern dress doing things that they could not have done in the earlier times, but to supply ideas and concepts missing from the traditional work. Even the appearance of the original designs would need to change—the choice of subjects and the way they are depicted had to be different from those of the 15th-century originators of Tarot.

In an age when psychology has become more of a guiding and motivating factor in our lives than religion, a modern Tarot must speak today's language, allowing for the fact that we understand and react to symbolism differently than in the Renaissance period. *The Fool's New Journey Tarot* avoids mis-readings of its symbolic language by representing recognizable aspects of the human condition without losing the deeper resonance of traditional Tarot. The art, too, is very different from that of earlier times—simpler, more direct, and more personal than the antique style of Renaissance art—which, beautiful and rich though it is, does not always speak to us as we need when seeking answers to modern issues.

As I had these thoughts in mind, a new collection of cards began to appear, largely intuitively, but always with deep con-templation. They included cards such as *Truth, The Listeners, The Remembering, The Forgetting,* and *Nature,* along with *Wisdom, The Clown,* and *The Observer.* In the end there were sixty, including all the original Major Arcana, which are far too important to lose, but with the addition of 38 new titles.

This left the Minor Arcana seemingly defunct, and I de-cided, not without a great deal of soul-searching, to drop these entirely. At the same time, a completely new sequence emerged, retaining the original Majors, but scattered through the se-quence of new cards, and including many of the original pip-card meanings as well. As Caitlín Matthews has stated in her *Time Changers Tarot* (REDFeather, 2023):

> *The Major Arcana speak with the archetypal voice that governs all beings on earth. Each card will automatically show you the bigger, collective picture of your question, revealing where the larger influences are at work within it. These may erupt into your life as irresistible forces of fate, as prevailing conditions that govern the world, or as influences that cause you to change or struggle. But they can also reveal to you the power to deal with current problems and dilemmas, how that power can help you withstand troubles, and how a community can harness the virtues that each major arcana offers.*

This was exactly the sense I was feeling from the new sequence of cards. The influence of powers beyond the range of our immediate senses represented everything that I felt was necessary for the influence of the new Tarot to express.

Tarot never had a single creator, but each generation has contributed to what it has become. Taking on a resetting of the familiar Major and Minor sequences was, from the start, a formidable task. But once the steps to remove the minor cards had been taken, the sequence fell quite quickly into place. Much time was spent considering the order of the rest. Early on I realised that the new cards had to be interleaved with the old, and that the first card would still be *The Fool*, since his journey though the sequence remains at the heart of modern Tarot. He would remain without a number, as he needed to be separate at some level from the rest of the pack. The last card would remain *The World*. But as the sequence grew and developed, it was felt that the meanings should transcend even this, and so *Eternity* was added as card 59. In rearranging the sequence, connections were looked for between cards, links that extend the possibilities of reading considerably.

Having reached this point, there followed over three years working with artist Charles Newington, whose take on the idea was wonderful. I asked him to strip out as much of the traditional imagery as possible and to keep the pictures simple. Sketches began to appear, which were beautiful and simple but packed a punch. From there, we went on playing with the images until we both were satisfied and felt they reflected the newer imagery. By this time, I had decided that a new sequence was required to completely sever the ties with the older decks. Some would remain in their normal places. To begin with, the working title was simply *The Reset Tarot*. This elided into *The Tabula Rasa Tarot*, suggesting the blank sheet on which the new ideas could be written. Finally, after much discussion, my wife plucked *The Fool's New Journey* out of the air, and everything felt it had fallen into place.

To make this even clearer—both to myself and the readers and users of this Tarot—I set out to write two stories, each one based on the idea of the Fool's Journey. The first is based on the original, classic Tarot trumps, the second on this new sequence. This proved to be an amazingly enlightening process. It taught me things that I thought I knew already about the Tarot as a whole, and specifically showed me how the original and the new sequence differed—and how they met and overlapped. I strongly suggest you read these before you begin working formally with *The Fool's New Journey Tarot*, as they are also a really good way to learn both the new sequence and the underlying meanings of each card for yourself.

What follows here is a new look at Tarot, literally a new journey for The Fool, resetting the style and purpose of the deck more or less back to zero, then taking it to places it has never been before. Some of the new cards will be seen to have grown out of the old, separating certain aspects of the original meanings into separate categories. For example, *The Worker* features aspects of the *7 and 8 of Pentacles,* while the old *4 of Swords* flows into *The Sleeper*, and the *3 of Swords* has become part of the meaning of *The Sorrowful. The Tower* is still present, with modern references added, but also includes aspects of *The Downfall*. Others are completely new, shifting the focus of meanings into previously unacknowledged areas of human experience.

I remain as much of a devotee of the original Tarot as I have been since I bought my first deck over 50 years ago. Here I offer something different—in the belief that users and readers may find it at once challenging and enlightening. Here begins The Fool's New Journey. Will you follow this path into a place of wisdom and discovery?

John Matthews
Oxford, 2022

PART
ONE

THE 60 TRIUMPHS:
MEANING AND INTERPRETATION

TAROT FOOL

Fool sings poems
To a broken lyre,
Dances on the bridge
With the rainbow spire.

Fool in Tarot
Lives the dream,
Follows in the footsteps
Of the dancing Queen.

Fool *is* Tarot
On sunny days,
Following the road
Through the glinting rays.

Fool on his journey
Never looks back,
Keeps on walking
On the ancient track.

Fool's every one of us
On our journeys too,
Fool keeps fooling us
With what is true.

So, what exactly is the Fool's Journey? As mentioned previously, the term was coined by Tarot aficionado Eden Grey in the 1950s, but it has perhaps always been present beneath the surface of classical Tarot. The Fool is always numbered 0 to distinguish him from the rest of the sequence. A layout of the major cards in the traditional sequence places him at the head, with all the rest of the cards below him:

The Fool's Traditional Journey (photo Dwina Gibb)

The journey that the Fool undertakes is one that we are all engaged upon—the journey of life itself. The fool is seen as an innocent, a blank slate upon which everything he or she experiences is written. Thus, the Fool's "new" journey, like the one he or she undertakes for us each time we make a reading, begins afresh. The road taken is filled with wisdom, terror, love, joy, and many other things—each of which we have, or will, experience in our own journeys. If you look carefully at the new sequence of cards—all triumphs (trumps) or Major Arcana—you will see that many tell an ongoing story. Not just your story—though you will find that there also—but the story of everyone. Not just a single story either, but several, which interleave with each other as the cards themselves do when shuffled—each story adding to another, building a new picture from which we may learn. If seeking specific answers, you will see how these emerge from the imagery and meanings of each card—joined together by the movement of one with another, showing your own part in the eternal dance of life. Read the two versions of the Fool's Journey (see part 2) to get an idea of how this works.

To begin with, if you are familiar with classic Tarot, you may find the new sequence less easy to read. The answer to this is simply a matter of getting to know the deck, familiarising yourself with the images and meanings. Some may be more obvious to you than others, but after spending a little time with each card (just as you would with any new deck) and considering the imagery of each, they should begin to open themselves to you. The stories will help with this. If you are a regular reader of the Tarot, you may find some of the traditional meanings changed—this is all part of the "new" journey undertaken by The Fool. These extended meanings are designed to interact with the new cards, together forming a powerful range of emotion and feeling with which each reader can interact. Take your time to familiarise yourself with the whole of the deck—don't just skip over the traditional cards, because some of these will have changed to better relate them to the new imagery. The less you compare these with the older traditions, the better, though there will be some overlaps and references that you will recognise. If you are a beginner, so much the better, as you will bring to the cards your own first impressions of their inherent meanings and their relationship to you and your own life journey.

With these thoughts in mind, let us take our first steps on *The Fool's New Journey* into discovery and wisdom—finding our own path laid out before us, and many fresh new meanings to help us divine the answers we seek.

Here, then, is a list of the 60 cards, followed by entries that include the meaning, any additional background information required, and lists of keywords for both upright and reversed reading. Following this, in the third part of this book, you will find methods of working, meditating, and reading the cards created especially for *The Fool's New Journey Tarot*.

. . .

0: The Fool

1: The Maze

2: The Believer

3: The Shadow

4: The Magician

5: The Priestess

6: Tradition

7: The Empress

8: The Emperor

9: The Hierophant

10: Wonder

11: Beauty

12: The Lovers

13: The Wasteland

14: The Chariot

15: Justice

16: The Prisoner

17: The Hanged Man

18: The Escape

19: The Hermit

20: The Sleep

21: The Dreamer

22: Strength

23: The Fisherman

24: The Teacher

25: The Worker

0: THE FOOL

The Fool is an ancient figure, first making a recorded appearance in classical Rome, where foolish characters were employed to behave in a carefree or wild manner both for the entertainment of the nobility and as a reminder not to take life too seriously. During the Middle Ages, fools or court jesters fulfilled a similar role and were given licence to be rude, crude, and silly for the entertainment of all. This continued throughout the Renaissance, when The Fool first appeared in the early Tarot decks, usually under the name *Le Mat* or *Il Matto*, both of which translate as "madman" or "beggar," giving the figure a moral or social significance not seen before. It was in the early 20th century that The Fool achieved the significance he still holds to this day—that of the one who begins a journey that represents us all. Indeed The Fool is everyone whose journey—both old and new—echoes our own, whose path we may follow or avoid (not always willingly), and whose end is unknowable until it is reached.

Eternally standing on the edge of beginning, The Fool is innocence, unknowingness, uncertainty—yet filled with untouched knowledge and unspoken truth. He or she is contradiction itself, setting out across a blank page where writing appears beneath each footfall. He or she is the primary seeker, the first to step forward, filled with the joys of life, which are explored without preconception or plan. Clouds may float above them, but, as here, he or she also contains the clouds, which, like them, are innocent. He or she is you and I as we set out upon any new venture. Plans may go awry, paths diverge, beliefs be shaken, traditions unstrung—yet we continue, blithely determined to find meaning where it may not exist, ever hopeful and every ready with a smile, a laugh, and a song. In doing so, we discover new things, answers we never thought to find, or even that they existed. Paths open on all sides, and provided that we have the qualities needed, we will travel far and learn great wisdom. Even without this, our journey is likely to be bright and full of unexpected delights. We dance the dance of The Fool no matter what it brings, no matter where we are. We are The Fool. The journey is ours.

Reversed, The Fool is foolish in another way. Seeing what is before them but stepping out regardless. He or she forgets to look where they are going; they move thoughtlessly across the blank page, stepping in the still-wet ink, leaping from page to page with careless abandon, smudging the words until they become senseless. As with the upright position, this is a card of beginnings, journeys, adventure, and wonder.

Keywords Upright: Innocence. Unknowingness. Crazy wisdom. Seeking. Change. The unexpected. Beginnings. Willingness to explore. To stay balanced on the narrow way.

Keywords Reversed: Thoughtlessness. Blasé behaviour. Carelessness. Uncertainty. Wildness. Adventure. Lack of preparation

1: THE MAZE

The Maze has been around for almost as long as there have been human beings. The oldest are found carved on rocks in various parts of the world. In almost every case, their meaning is clear: they are about getting lost, about finding the way again, about testing oneself to see how far we can go and how we can respond to random events, while moving through the maze. The most famous maze of all was that built by the great artificer Daedalus in Greek myth. It was made to house the monstrous Minotaur, half man and half bull, to which sacrifices were made every year. This serves to show that the maze can be both a trap as well as a means of understanding a part of life that we are not clear about. In more recent times the maze has become known as a symbol not only for life's (or The Fool's) journey, but also for the brain. Our own human brain, like that of many mammals, resembles a maze, and in its coils is hidden our true self. The Fool, like many of us when we undertake a journey of discovery, has no idea where it will take us—or if we do, which route it will take. Medieval mazes were built mostly by monks of the Benedictine order, who often constructed them to serve as symbolic pilgrim routes. Someone who longed, for instance, to reach the holy city of Jerusalem could do so symbolically by following the shape of a maze on their knees—hence the large number of turf mazes found close to monastic sites. The Maze then is both a catalyst of possibilities and a place in which we can lose our way. In a reading, it can be read as positive or negative, making it a truthful representation of the road taken.

Reversed, The Maze can mean an overconfidence in our ability to find a way or the answer to our issues. We may enter The Maze believing we will reach the centre, but sometimes we forget the need to depart, not always by the same route we came in by. Also, problems tend to gather at the centre of The Maze unless we are strong enough, and clever enough, to escape them. We may find ourselves lost amid the many turnings, unable to get free. Only careful consideration of choices can give us the ability to depart.

Keywords Upright: Lost. Confused. Wandering. Uncertainty. Inability to choose. Doubt. Taking the long way to your goals.

Keywords Reversed: Too much confidence in finding the way. Arrogance. Determination in the face of doubt. Looking for truths that are not there. Not noticing the way ahead.

2: THE BELIEVER

The Believer is one who seeks to believe in whatever can best strengthen him or her. Belief is, and always has been, a two-edged sword. On the one hand, it can be a simple belief in oneself; on the other, a foundation for the tenets of a religion or tradition. It becomes darker when we become slaves of a particular path, unable to accept change or to break the mold of older times. Belief in the self is essential to progress of any kind, though that too can become inflexible and cloud the wisdom of the free heart and mind. Belief in others, or in a good cause, gives us a sense of purpose essential to life, but even then the best intentions can be overturned by a slavish determination that the subject of our belief—be it individual or creed—blocks the way and makes slaves of us. Taken at a simple human level, it is wise to believe in yourself, but less so to become so dominated by your own unassailable truth that you cease to listen to others. Thus, you should believe in your ability to succeed, to grow strong, to survive the hardest issues of life, but also remain clear that you can allow yourself to be free of constraints and follow your own path. Belief in a religion is equally fraught with problems. We see this every day when we hear of a religious leader who imposes a system of belief on everyone, to the exclusion of thought, will, or clear-sightedness. For such people there is no room for question or doubt—things that we need if we are to survive. Like The Fool on the edge of the cliff, we must learn to dance on the thin line between believing and questioning.

Reversed, this card speaks of becoming trapped in a world of absolutes that give no room to asking if this is the right way forward. All too often we become trapped in the words and ideas of those who believe without questioning. This can be comforting, especially in times of grief or challenge, but it is always a dangerous path that can lead to doing what we are told without concern for others, or indeed for our own free will.

Keywords Upright: Faith. The cause. Activism. Certainty. Following your heart. Belief in the self. Acknowledging more than one truth.

Keywords Reversed: Unquestioning acceptance. Entrapment. Servitude. Blindness. Uncaring. Sticking to the path. Having no self-awareness.

3: THE SHADOW

Shadows are extraordinary. They follow us, attend us, and occasionally mock us. When Peter Pan loses his shadow, he becomes unnatural. Shadows can be creepy, exciting, mysterious, or joyful. Watch your shadow dance with you and you'll find it virtually impossible not to feel happy. But The Shadow is something more. It's a part of ourselves that we all know, but which most of us try hard not to acknowledge or experience—though we feel its presence within us. It may be a darker, more negative part of our being, which seeks gratification without concern for others. It is also a place, a turning on the road that we may find ourselves upon whether we like it or not. It encourages us to see the darker side of any situation, to take a more selfish and negative approach to whatever issue arrives. It is often faceless, as we have pictured it here. It tells us that we are hidden from the light and that the darkness is more welcoming; yet, without light there can be no shadow! Be careful of giving into the darkness, as you may find yourself getting lost amid the gloom and stuck on a negative path. Remember too that it is a part of you, whether you like it or acknowledge it or feel it is a part you would prefer did not exist. The objective of life is to become whole and to remain whole, complete with negative aspects as well as positive. Darkness is no more negative than light—both have a part to play in all that you experience in your lifetime.

Reversed, The Shadow is protective, preventing us from becoming blinded by the light. It tells you that your personal confidence is strong and stable, that all new attempts will lead to even better things. However, situations can be misleading and can lead you astray, just as this may happen with an upright reading.

Keywords Upright: Gloom. Uncertainty. Lack of foresight. Fantasist leanings. Negativity. The glass half full. Failure to acknowledge your own negative side. Shape-shifting.

Keywords Reversed: Misalignment. Confusion. Negative light. Dreaming. Regression. Comfort. Hidden truths.

4: THE MAGICIAN

The Magician is traditionally a trickster, ever ready to baffle us with his sleight of hand, his almost magical link to the cards he deals. He is both clever and subtle and has been interpreted in this light as everything from a magus to a mountebank. The oldest form of this archetype is known as the Juggler and is generally depicted as a man dressed in harlequin costume, standing at a table and performing the infamous "three-cup trick," in which a pebble is supposedly hidden under one of three cups, which are then moved around quickly, and a member of the audience is asked to tell which one. Usually the stone is found easily enough the first or second time, but on the third it has been palmed so that the unlucky person loses everything. Here, we have shown this in action but given him the illusion of four arms with which to manoeuvre the cups as he wishes. He is also literally juggling, displaying the skill necessary to keep the cards in the air. But there is another side to this figure, which later resulted in his name being changed from Juggler to Magus or Magician. This is his subtlety, his ability to bamboozle the audience while actually performing genuine magic.

The card is often associated with the ego, the desire (and ability) to uncover the creativity of others. However, the archetype of The Magician here has more to do with being able to penetrate the outer shell of reality and to delve deeply into the heart of the matter. Here, the card has more to do with viewing the circumstances of a problem and seeing beyond them, of passing from a state of uncertainty to its opposite. The Magician causes things to happen. He may disguise himself in another form, but when revealed he is a powerful and effective figure, who in readings represents the innate strength of the reader to cause changes to occur at the subtlest levels of being.

Reversed, The Magician can represent a powerful figure with the ability to lead people astray or can simply indicate to the reader that they are, in a sense, fooling themselves. Here we enter a realm of uncertainty, where events are less clear than they need to be. The Magician changes destiny and reverses circumstances by engaging with them. We need to keep our eyes firmly on all the cards to ensure we are able to function properly. We must learn to look beyond appearances to recognise the reality that determines our future.

Keywords Upright: Skill. Willpower. Diplomacy. Cleverness. Trickery. Subtlety. Mind over matter. Certainty.

Keywords Reversed: Deceit. Falsehood. Manipulation. Chicanery. Illusion. Indecision. Exploitation.

5: THE PRIESTESS

The Priestess has been, at various times, identified with the Egyptian goddess Isis, the Roman Sibyl, and, in more recent times, a pagan High Priestess. We have simplified her title to refer more to one who acts as mediator and focaliser, but in other ways her role remains essentially unchanged. In most of the early representations of the figure, she possesses a great book, to which she may be pointing or turning outward as if inviting the viewer to read the page she has opened. Here we have presented her with the spiral of knowledge, the crown of the divine mysteries, and the lunar magic of the feminine. Her arms are crossed in thoughtfulness, and to indicate clear boundaries. Her power is unquestioned and her strength is of the deepest and most profound kind. She is, in some ways, the feminine power that men flee from, unable to deal with its strength and purity, which far outstrips their own intellectual pursuits. Her presence often indicates a strong and powerful woman whose advice may well be important, but whose influence can be overwhelming. Some portraits show her sitting with her feet on the moon, and here she clearly displays this moon-powered, intuitional wisdom that governs her influence in the readings where she appears.

Reversed, though her wisdom is deep and sensitive, it can also, in a more negative context, suggest an inability to act, to turn wisdom into action. She can also lead seekers astray with suggestions that encourage pride and selfishness, and she may also suggest passion out of control, consuming those who experience it. At her best she is a light that leads the way to greater wisdom; at worst she is a nagging, insensitive gossip.

Keywords Upright: Wisdom. Mediator. Inward looking. Visionary. The subconscious. Intuition. Depths. Teaching. Self-sufficiency. The Sacred. Fertility of imagination.

Keywords Reversed: Selfishness. Ignorance. Self-doubt. Intrigue. Gossip. Misjudgement in time of crisis. False direction. Secretiveness.

6: TRADITION

Tradition can be many things. It holds memories of the past and teaches us to look around us in directions we may not normally consider. As the poet T. S. Eliot wrote, "We have become the bearers of tradition." But tradition is not just about the past or carrying its burdens. It can be said that we make new traditions every day, and these leave deep marks in our hearts and minds. Tradition is, indeed, a carrier; it holds the wisdom of our ancestors that did not always make it into written form. It is one of the great tools of learning because it enshrines so much that might otherwise be lost. Sometimes it can become burdensome too, holding us in a grip that speaks of immovable ways of doing things—simply because it's "a tradition." So, while we should honour traditions, both old and new, we should be careful not to become hidebound. Traditions must adapt as well as remaining strong and purposeful. As yourself you might ask, What traditions do I follow? Is it something I still need to adhere to as strictly as I have? The new approach to Tarot embodied in this deck is a prime example; there is a long and worthy tradition regarding the number of cards and their names and symbols. In breaking with that tradition, we have not given away the value of the older forms, just adapted and expanded them for our own and future times. In the end, you can learn much wisdom from tradition, but it is still advisable not to become its slave.

Reversed, tradition can be a powerful master that demands complete surrender. We can very easily fall into the habit of sticking with tradition because our parents and grandparents did, or because we seek to honor our ancestors. This of itself is no bad thing, but it can become a trap and should be watched out for.

Keywords Upright: Traditional ways. Old beliefs. Considered truths. Free flowing tides of knowledge. Wisdom of other times. Ways of learning.

Keywords Reversed: Blindly accepting the past. Hidebound thinking. Failing to acknowledge the new. Sticking to old patterns. Unwillingness to grow and transform.

7: THE EMPRESS

The Empress can be said to complete the feminine energy represented by The Priestess. Where the former brings wisdom, The Empress brings strength, and holds within her the qualities of rulership and command. Between her hands she balances the sphere of passionate honesty, elements of which are present in all her readings. In the oldest Tarot decks she was very simply a ruler, but from the 19th century onward, her more mystical aspect became the focus—she is now more often seen as "the Woman Clothed in the Sun and crowned with stars" from the biblical book of Revelation, while the more esoteric interpreters refer to her as Isis-Urania—a composite figure focused upon by the 19th-century Order of the Golden Dawn. Urania means heavenly and was a title given to goddesses such as Venus. Many have seen her as either Venus or Aphrodite, the classical goddesses of love, and the stories of their capricious nature and nurture have become part of the meaning of the card. She can be seen to stand for every powerful female ruler from ancient times to the present. In our own time, she can be recognized as the powerful CEO of a company, a female prime minister, or the advisor to heads of government.

Unlike her sister, The Empress embodies human love—especially that of the mother, both of children and of all who live and walk and draw breath in this world. Her task is to watch over those who come to her, and her kindness manifests as maternal love. She is also the sovereign of romantic love and represents the passionate response between lovers. In a reading she may represent a strong female companion—wife, sister, daughter, or friend, whose earthy qualities lend themselves to support but can also overbalance the psyche by encouraging reckless behavior when reversed.

Reversed, she can signify a reliance on passion and emotion without due consideration. Her two strengths are the nurture she offers and the understanding of passionate relationships —but when reversed, these can overwhelm with smothering love. Anyone who has experience the destructive love of a mother who cares too much for her child will recognize The Empress and be wary of her, but to those who travel freely through life, she is boon companion whose caring nature is both protective and enlivening.

Keywords Upright: Abundance. Guardianship. Fertility. Ruling passions. Health. The feminine. Marriage. Embodiment. Wild nature. Nurture. Action.

Keywords Reversed: Smothering love. Recklessness. Infidelity. Inaction. Adultery.

8: THE EMPEROR

The Emperor, as in traditional Tarot, sits on his great throne, dispensing wisdom and power, balancing elements of both through his own innate qualities. He is, as many have noted before, like Solomon, the great biblical king who was also a magician and a prophet. The mighty French emperor Charlemagne may also be a contender for this role, as are the Byzantine emperors who inherited the wisdom of Greece and Rome. Above all, The Emperor represents stability. His appearance as the eighth card in the sequence of the Major Arcana (originally the fourth) suggests the "four-square" nature of his power. His throne is solid and monumental, and when he sits upon it, he enters into his power, manifesting it to all who come before him. Like The Empress, he can be both protective and aggressive—his guardianship, like that of a father, may sometimes seem harsh, though it is most often tempered with love. This is also the card of the leader, the one who takes charge and sorts out the problems by asserting authority and will.

Reversed, his judgement may be too summary, so certain is he of his innate power. In a reading, his presence indicates an authoritative father figure (actual or metaphorical) whose words should be weighed before accepting them. It suggests that the blind acceptance of the rules governing society should be tempered with reason and feeling—both concepts that may be lacking in The Emperor. If the question relates to the family, it may indicate a need to reassess the relationships between fathers and children. In every instance the circumstances require careful consideration, depending on the context. In all, be wary of powerful figures whose demeanor can become tyrannical.

Keywords Upright: Stability. Authority. Fatherhood. Intellect. Forward movement. Solidarity. Law. Reason. Conviction. Male authority. Accomplishment. Organiser. Regulation. Leadership.

Keywords Reversed: Instability. Authoritarianism. Misuse of power. Tyranny. Stubbornness. Immaturity.

9: THE HIEROPHANT

The Hierophant (literally "He Who Leads the Way") was originally titled The Pope until the 19th century, when the esoteric Order of the Golden Dawn changed it. Here, the figure radiates peaceful contemplation, the journey into contentment through the opening of doors, leading to ever-deepening knowledge. This is a being, person, or impulse whose wisdom is supreme, someone to whom you may turn unhesitatingly for advice and direction. Yet, there is also a sense—perhaps the product of our own times more than anything—that tempers the belief in this person's position of power with doubt and caution. In readings, the card usually reflects the presence of a strong figure in our lives or an institution to which we might turn for help or guidance. Yet, beyond this, we may see the glimmering of another possibility—an opportunity to find the truth and wisdom we seek within ourselves. Inevitably, given human nature's ability to misread or misinterpret ideas, this is a far-harder task than simply sitting at the feet of a wise being—inner or outer. But if we learn to look within as well as at outer influences in our lives, we will quickly find that answers still come. Then it is up to us to trust our own inner realizations.

Reversed, there is a very real danger in accepting guidance either from one who presents it to us, or indeed from our own inner realizations. Masters of wisdom, whether religious leaders or occult teachers, may seem all powerful and enlightened but have all too often been shown to have feet of clay. Like The Emperor, The Hierophant can be seen as a well-meaning but ultimately mistaken teacher or even a misguided parent. Sometimes we are guided to turn way from such authority figures, replacing their wisdom with our own. The card can and does represent personal convictions, or beliefs that outweigh the more established institutions such as organized religion. In such instances, it is up to us to follow our instinct.

Keywords Upright: Spiritual conviction or belief. Practitioner of high wisdom. Esoteric knowledge. Tradition. Inspiration. Marriage. Good advice. Mercy. Mediator. Guide. Way shower.

Keywords Reversed: Dogmatism. Hypocrisy. Weakness. Instability. Inflexible morality. Turning away from established truths.

10: WONDER

Wonder is a great though often-neglected requirement in everyday life. To live without it is to wander in a dark place. To experience wonder is to become aware of the beauty that surrounds us and to acknowledge its importance in our lives. Wonder can be many things: the sense of amazement upon recognising the true nature and imperishable value of people, places, or even things, and the sense of being filled with a sense of wonder toward all things, which both nourishes and sustains us daily. Look at the wonders that surround you: the rising and setting of the sun, the glitter of stars from an impossible distance, the tender delight in a child or adult who stands at the centre of your life. The reawakened desire to plunge into the depth of the ocean we call life, to follow its tides as they spin us into greater and greater awareness of the true meaning of existence. We need wonder. Without it we have no sense of wonderment, of questioning, without which life would be dull—because to wonder is also to question, and without questions there are no answers, no certainty (see also card 33: The Questioner). With Wonder we are encouraged to look past the surface appearances of things to appreciate their dynamic beauty. It opens the doors of the infinite and allows us to see past illusion to the miracles that surround us everywhere we look.

Reversed, the meaning can indicate loss of the wonder we already possess, or a misreading of appearances that may confuse the honest nature of everything around us. It can mean that we are prone to accept things as they are presented, without questioning or seeking to get to the heart of the subject. Without wonder, we have less understanding and may turn away from a direction that can lead us to a better state of being or mind.

Keywords Upright: A sudden revelation. Recognising the wonder of life. Acknowledging something greater than ourselves. A surprise. Being aware. Seeing into the heart of things. Wondering. Questioning.

Keywords Reversed: Unresponsive. Accepting easy solutions. Seeing nothing beyond the immediate and basic. Dullness. Unquestioning. Failing to recognise the wonder in life.

11: BEAUTY

Beauty? What do we mean by it? How do we judge it? What—or who—is beautiful to one may not be to another. The Wonder card possesses beauty and thus connects to the previous card. But the way in which we see beauty—how we judge it to be beautiful—is a very different thing. Just as Wonder is generally instinctual, Beauty is very much in the eye of the beholder. Beauty is both within and without. Sometimes the outer beauty does not reach the inner person, and at times those whose appearance does not fit our own idea of beauty live still within the person we turn away from. Yet, it is important that we acknowledge beauty—whatever we mean by it—because it affects so much of our life on a daily basis. Actions can be beautiful—creations often are, and of course those whom we love are always beautiful to us at the deepest level. Beauty is much more than that of an individual— it is also a feeling. A soul may be beautiful and may look out from the eyes of someone we know but that others do not recognise. Beauty stretches our perceptions, and to live a beautiful life takes every bit of strength and sense of who we are that we can muster. In a reading we ask: What is beautiful about this situation, or what is not, what is ugly and difficult and challenging? When we look at the shape of our journey, do we see an elegant series of curves and lines, or a maze of twisted, broken threads? Such considerations are all part of our understanding of beauty and of our journey. Nor should we forget the natural world that surrounds us wherever we are. Beauty is there also and warms us as we walk through the often-troublesome and often-painful events of daily life.

Reversed, Beauty may claim us in another way—we become enamoured of the glamorous and the unattainable, diverted from our life path into troubled waters. Not for nothing were the old magics of an earlier times referred to as "glamour." Long before the word meant what it does now, it meant a kind of magic that brought people to their knees and took away their individuality and self-worth. This kind of beauty is dangerous and destructive; it is best avoided lest you lose your way.

Keywords Upright: Physical or spiritual beauty. Harmony and grace. Wholeness. Integrity. Poise. Beauty of place, or creativity, of life itself.

Keywords Reversed: Beauty beheld. Beauty hidden. Beauty overwhelming. Loss of stability of the observer. Loss of feelings. Hopeless longings. Superficial.

12: THE LOVERS

The Lovers are as many and varied as clouds in the sky. The symbolism of this card has always been, at heart, the idea of both divine and human love in all its forms. Though the lovers depicted here could be any one of a dozen famous couples—Lancelot and Guinevere, Dante and Beatrice, Tristan and Isolde, Apollo and Adonis, Achilles and Patroclus, they are more than this. They represent all lovers, including those of every gender and kind, not just those whose amorous feelings are of the human persuasion. Here, love is also that of mankind for its gods, and of its gods for humanity. In classical myth, love was ruled by Eros (or Cupid), whose arrows were tipped either with gold or lead. The golden arrows produced instant infatuation in the heart of those it pierced; the lead brought the exact opposite—loathing. Thus the god was said to be impartial, and many early Tarots represent three figures, suggesting the torment of having to decide between two loves. Beyond this, references are not only to romantic and sexual passion but to love of family, siblings, work, place, and pleasures such as music, books, and art. It is often related to adolescent love, which is more powerful in its ability to overwhelm. On another level still, it refers to the more remote and transformative love of the divine and the interaction between humans and gods. The card has always had a lot to do with choice—indeed, that is an alternative name for this trump—and love triangles are often depicted as an underlying meaning. In every case, Love itself, Eros, watches over those whom his darts have struck, and in any reading concerned with romantic love, the implication points to the presence of help and hope.

Reversed, uncertainty and instability accompanying its more obvious meanings. In most readings the card serves literally to "marry" the meanings of the cards that surround it, and the communication inherent in its upright position becomes the opposite when reversed. Thus it may indicate separation, even divorce, though not only of a marriage but from friends or workmates, tasks or hopes. People fall in and out of love all the time, and this card can indicate either a burgeoning romance or the end of a relationship. The thread here is of disunity rather than closeness, loss rather than gain. Everything should be weighed in the balance before making an irrevocable decision.

Keywords Upright: Love. Relationship. Intimacy. Choice. Fate. Unity. Clarity. Kindness. Agreement. Passion impulse. Harmony. Trials overcome. Optimism. Trust. Choice.

Keywords Reversed: Separation. Divorce. Unsettled life. Reversals. Disharmony. Uncertainty. Disunity. Breaking apart. Unhappiness. Failure of love. Obsession.

13: THE WASTELAND

The Wasteland is the place we make when we forget the meaning of life and take up the dark path of warfare and destruction. This destroys not only life, but also the land, and the message it sends to others is that we care only for dominance and power over others. Life ceases to matter. Destruction is everywhere. Within ourselves, as individuals, it kills our future and arrests any development that might be welcomed in our hearts. The wounds of the earth are our wounds, whether we feel responsible for them or not. Here we see the detritus of countless wars—ancient helmets, modern bombs, broken ruins. Whatever the weapons—and these may be words, gestures, and patterns of action—the results are almost always the same. One side triumphs, but the losers wither. Nor are there guarantees that the "good" side will win. Only the first signs of new growth on the vestigial, dystopian tree give a reason for hope.

The ancient myth of the Wasteland comes from within the mysteries of the Grail, sought by King Arthur's knights in the beginning and by countless seekers after truth ever since. In the stories there are different causes for the Wasteland. Sometimes the otherworldly women who guarded and pro-tected the Cup were attacked and the vessel stolen by evil men. In other versions the guardian of the Grail is a king who receives a wound that will not heal until the Grail is recovered. When he receives healing, so does the land, for kings anciently married the land and became partner to it rather than ruling over it. In the individual this speaks of a deeply hidden sorrow for which there seems no cure; yet, we have hope, and if our will allows us, we can search for healing for ourselves. So too if we feel we are stagnating, unable to move either forward or back, we can seek the strength that enables us to break the bonds of loss, of hopelessness and fear that bind us in the darkest of circumstances. In a larger sense, we see here the failure of our duty to our environment, our inability to feel how the land can be torn apart just as we ourselves—both physically and spiritually—can become broken by anger, frustration, and a hated of others.

Reversed, we may see ways in which we can restore the Waste-land, looking amid the reality of our lives, the wreckage of lost opportunity, failure in love or intent, instead seeing the true value of the gifts we possess within ourselves and the hidden strength that allows us to crawl out of the dark and begin the work of restoration—both upon ourselves and the lands around us. This tells us not to look for disaster and doubt, but to flourish and grow green like the land itself after the desolation of winter. The tree grows again in the midst of barrenness.

Keywords Upright: Desolation. Destruction. Stagnation. Loss of direction. Loss of purpose. Abandonment. Environmental failure. Old wounds. Madness.

Keywords Reversed: Recovery. Restoration. Resolve. Finding healing for old wounds. New growth. Recognition. Using gifts wisely.

14: THE CHARIOT

The Chariot is all about movement. It is the very representation of motion, forward or back, of the driver in the seat who commands the way, knows what direction to take, and delivers what is needed to deal with whatever situation arises. The journeys we take, like that of The Fool, require the harnessing of both the will and the emotions, without which all actions are impulsive and may even be dangerous. The heart as well as the head must rule if one is to obtain one's desires, and mastery over the worldly life and the ability to transcend everyday concerns is central to its understanding. The twin horses of emotion and intellect, disharmony and calm, require balance, enabling progress to be undertaken with fewer of the stresses and strains of everyday life. Consider how hard you work to build your career, winning fame and creating influence around you. Mastery of skill or ability brings a successful outcome; self-confidence and self-discipline enable the harnessing of abilities. Navigating life with a clear sense of direction ensures that you arrive at a solution to the problem before others. You make a great leap forward with your hands on the reins. Success and fame are the rewards of achievement, so be prepared to handle them.

However, before you can win any race, you must first win the trust of the horses that pull the vehicle, which, in their untamed state, tend to pull in opposite directions. Look therefore to bring others into play, forming a team that you can steer toward your goal. But be careful not to allow too much desire for control to warp your judgement. At the heart of a determined progression toward any goal exists a calm center. If you enter this state of being, the way becomes altogether smoother.

Reversed, the card represents disharmony brought about by a determination to press ahead without thought or care for others. Loss of control, rage, and a failure to seek a harmonious solution to problems follow. This emphasizes the situation where horses are left to themselves, causing the chariot to spin out of control. Feelings of anger and frustration are also indicated, as is the inability to move forward. Familiar paths may lead to unexpected places. Overconfidence can be deflated by failure.

Keywords Upright: Movement. Journey. Harmony. The need for emotional control. Trouble overcome. Harnessing emotion and will. Triumph. Mastery. Control. Progress.

Keywords Reversed: Stasis. Failure. Defeat. Conquest. Quarrel. Bad news. Too much ambition. Disputation. Failure. Accident. Concern. Opportunism. Rebellion. Feeling lost.

15: JUSTICE

Justice wears no blindfold and sees into the depth of our hearts, requiring us to do the same. She requires of us to be honest with ourselves and our issues, that we acknowledge the truth of our lives and act accordingly. Only by following this precept is the truth allowed to emerge. In other words, if we live with a desire to see the truth in everything, then truth is what we will see, but if we live with a sense of bias, we will experience everything in this light and remain out of balance. For this reason alone, the card is crucial to any reading. What it offers us is a true statement about the issue in hand. It is, in effect, a just assessment of the situation, to which we should pay the utmost attention.

Scattered throughout the sequence of the traditional Greater Arcana are figures that represent the four cardinal virtues of humanity—Justice is one of these, along with Fortitude, Temperance, and Prudence. Originally listed by Plato, they were considered to be the foundational concepts that raised mankind above the level of the animal kingdom. Christianity later added three more: Faith, Hope, and Charity, creating a moral framework upon which humanity could build a stable world. Justice ranked the highest among all of these, as she was believed to balance the scales of fate in such a manner that all who followed her received their just deserts—according to the way of life they lived. Earlier echoes of the archetype point to the goddess Astraea, who according to Greek myth lived on the earth during the golden age but, as humanity became increasingly wicked, withdrew to live among the heavens, from where she could oversee the provision of Justice to all. The symbolism is clear enough: justice is meted out impartially, according to the life lived; the flower may be cut down at any time.

Reversed, we may realise that we are refusing to perceive a situation honestly, preferring to perceive it from our own, selfish, point of view. This often results in blaming everyone and everything for things we have ourselves caused. In readings concerned with relationships, either personal or professional, it indicates a need to be absolutely fair in your dealings. Justice is impartial and requires us to be the same. If your concern is with your own personal progress through life, it may indicate a need to reassess your approach and to acknowledge that the problems you are facing may be of your own causing. Nor should you forget that beyond the personal, the notion of justice and fairness is something we can personally implement in our dealings with the rest of the world.

Keywords Upright: Balance. Fairness. Justice for all. Harmony. Virtuousness. Honour. Impartiality. A fair outcome. Equilibrium. Law. Discovering the truth. Self-knowledge. Even-handedness.

Keywords Reversed: Bias. False witness. Bigotry. Intolerance. Unfairness. Red tape. Blindness to the truth. Out of balance. Selfish behaviour.

16: THE PRISONER

The Prisoner represents that part of us that feels trapped, held fast and unmoving behind bars. The famous series of pictures by the artist Giovanni Piranesi (1720–1778), *Caerceri* (*Prisons*), show vast dark places hung with chains and webs connected by paths that lead nowhere. Following any one of these simply brings us back to where we began. These are things we are just as likely to create for ourselves as to refer to the more literal understanding of imprisonment. Of course we may see some links with the preceding card, Justice, where the sentence imposed following wrongdoing is to be imprisoned. But these are literal and tangential. Here we focus on the kinds of imprisonment that we often create for ourselves. As we progress on our own journeys, we will, unless we are supremely lucky, find ourselves taking a wrong turn, being forced into a situation where we cannot move either forward or back. Opposing ideas and beliefs, as well as the actions of others, bring us to a point of stasis. We literally cannot move in any direction and may feel disempowered by our surroundings and those with power over us. In a reading, this card may describe your own current situation and suggest helplessness. We must look to the cards that precede or follow it to see what options are available. Often this means taking a step away from the turmoil of the situation, so that we can better observe both cause and effect.

Reversed, the card may express, on one level, freedom itself, a sense of lightness as we emerge from a dark place back into the sun. It also suggests a willingness to let go of the things that bind us, so that we are no longer trapped by them. Old patterns of behaviour often hold us in their grip, and freedom means separating from these and looking to new paths. It is about the recovery of life rather than its loss.

Keywords Upright: Imprisonment. Feeling trapped. Loss of freedom. Loss of agency. Loss of identity.

Keywords Reversed: Released. Breaking out. Freedom from old patterns. Recovering life.

17: THE HANGED MAN

The Hanged Man has had many interpretations. For some his role is positive, offering fresh insights by enabling us to literally see things from upside down. For others, he represents someone caught between events, unable to move or find a good outcome. But The Hanged Man is not dead, but merely suspended between heaven and Earth. He may also have freely offered himself to be hung up in this fashion. The meaning of the card can thus refer either to a turning away from traditional values, sometimes more starkly rendered as treachery, for the Man hangs by one foot, his head toward the earth, drawn away from the high principles of heaven toward the darker feelings of the underworld. This is a complex card for a number of reasons. It is notoriously ambiguous as to its exact meaning, and as it is already "upside down," reversals work differently to normal traditional interpretation that describes it as about getting stuck, literally hung up and unable to proceed at all, either backward or forward, as in the case of card 16: The Prisoner, showing that the two are related. It has also acquired a connection with drug abuse, and with any addiction that has an unbreakable hold on the user. There is also a sense of transition here; the figure hangs between one moment and the next and may fall to the earth or be pulled upward in the heavens. Nor should we forget that as the man hangs between heaven and Earth, he may receive visions and fresh insights that can help him find balance once his feet touch the ground.

Reversed, there is a subtly different, more positive side to the card. In the original images the face of the hanged figure is always serene, implying that he has mastered his passions or addictions and come to terms with life. We have followed this idea here, giving him a serene and untroubled look, aware of all possibilities and willing to follow where they may lead. The card in a reading suggests that the best course of action may sometimes be to do nothing, and that rather than seeing this as a negative, passive solution, it may point to a wisdom that transcends the situation. However, we must also be wary of behaving selfishly and striking out blindly at those we think have done us wrong. Promises made may be forgotten by either side, of making hasty, ill-judged decisions that will be detrimental to both ourselves and others.

Keywords Upright: Transition. New insights. Reversals. Change. Rebirth. Sacrifice. Intuition. Prophecy. Acceptance. Stuck. Indecision. Sacrifice. Addiction.

Keywords Reversed: Selfishness. Stunted thinking. Failure to make the right decision. Failed promises. Egotism. Unjust accusations. Addiction. Being stuck. Reversals.

18: THE ESCAPE

The Escape may sound like running away, but in fact it is about letting go, allowing yourself to escape from the constraints you have placed around yourself. Allied with the card of The Prisoner, it connects with the moment when you discover the way to release yourself from your entanglements.

On our journey through life, we often encounter points where we are forced to face up to overwhelming situations. Sometimes we have to step away from these in order to see them more clearly in the light of other events going on around us. Making a quick decision may not be a great idea in such circumstances, and we may come to regret this later. Instead, if we can, we might take a break from the issue and give ourselves a few days away from the cliff face in order to reconsider. We even use the term "escape" for this very purpose, without seeing it as a bad or cowardly thing. Often, simply stepping back, taking a broader view, and then returning refreshed to the situation can make a world of difference. You may think this a platitude, but try it before you become overwhelmed, and remember that your energies need harbouring from time to time.

Reversed, you need to be careful of not emulating the figure of Icarus from Greek myth, who donned wings constructed by his father, the great artificer Daedalus, to escape the imprisonment of the maze at Knossos. The pride he felt at this achievement caused him to fly too close to the sun, so that the wax holding his wings together melted and he fell into the sea. This may seem an extreme notion, but we need to be just as careful not to abandon our position as we should, too wary of sticking to the post for longer than is required. Consider your options with care as you read this card, and be aware of those that flank it on either side.

Keywords Upright: Gaining freedom and agency. Breaking the chains that bind. Leaving a situation behind. Retreating to reconsider your situation.

Keywords Reversed: Abandoning your position. Seeking peace before solving the outstanding issue. Becoming caught up in lesser events.

19: THE HERMIT

The Hermit may suggest the idea of someone who dwells in solitary isolation, contemplating the events of the world, or of his/her life, and seeking a resolution to all. But the Hermit of the Tarot is no ordinary character—as the alternative names of "the Old One" and "the Devourer of Things" indicate. In fact, the earliest Tarot images identify him with the figure of Time, or sometimes the Roman god Saturn, who preceded him. This completely changes the seemingly benign figure of The Hermit into a far more serious proposition. Since time is generally seen as the great enemy of humanity, the one who rolls up life and, in the end, takes it away, he is a figure demanding our attention. The Hermit contemplates the passage of events in order to find a true meaning but also acknowledges the passage of time and the way this impacts upon the issues under consideration. Such acknowledgment allows the seeker to be detached, enabling a clearer view of the circumstances that have brought the problem into being. Sometimes this card in a reading suggests the presence of a teacher or guide who shows us how to reach a point of stillness that enables us to see more clearly what action to take. For this reason, The Hermit is also seen as representing transition, prophecy, and insightful detachment.

Reversed, there is a darker side to the card, indicating that we love our own company too much and are becoming isolated from reality, or blind to the reality of our situation. Self-awareness, the acknowledgment of the real place we have reached in our journey through life, almost always triggers change. From the moment the pendulum's swing reaches a point of rest, the only thing that can follow is motion. The card thus suggests movement away from stasis, a triumphant return to a path abandoned—a deepening of awareness of the goals of life. But to reach this, we may have to enter into a period of withdrawal, and it is important to keep a finger on the pulse of life in case we become caught in the circle of time and lose our way. Failure to do this can lead to imprudent actions.

Keywords Upright: Bringing light. Solitariness. A retreat. Seeking illumination. Meditation. A seeker after truth. Time. Honesty. Prudent awareness. Caution. Prophecy. Detachment. Freedom of action. Maturity.

Keywords Reversed: Isolation. Blindness. Opposition. Imprudence. Immaturity. Withdrawal from the world. Thoughtlessness.

20: THE SLEEP

Sleep is something we cannot live without; yet, our approach to it is ambiguous. Some fear sleep for the nightmares it can bring, while others welcome it as a cessation of the troubles and stresses of daily life. It is a source of refreshment and refuelling and, via our dreams, leads us to discover things we may not otherwise know about (see card 21: The Dreamer). Myths are full of references to the guardians of sleep, gods and goddesses who guide us though dream or vision to partake of a larger wisdom and wider world. In the Greek pantheon, the god of sleep is Hypnos, while in Rome he is named Morpheus (the Fashioner) because of his skill at being able to take upon himself the form of other beings or people. According to the poet Ovid (43 BCE–17 CE), "No other is more skilled than he in representing the walk, features, and speech of men; so too he copies the clothing and even the familiar words of those he represents." The poet gives Morpheus two brothers, saying that they appear in dreams "mimicking many forms." These "sons of sleep" are Phobetor ("the Frightener"), who is able to take the form of beast or bird or of a serpent, and Phanatos ("Fantasy"), who "takes upon him the deceptive shapes of earth, rock, water, and trees." These all speak of the ways in which sleep can become filled with people we believe we know, but who may actually be wearing masks. These are something more than dreams and are capable of showing us things we fail to recognise in everyday life. In a reading the card may suggest our need take more care to observe events around us and try to recognise their true value. It also points to a need for rest and restoration, to take a break from the busy lives we lead.

Reversed, the card points to a craving for sleep that nonetheless does not deliver the respite we need. Sleep without refreshment, or indeed an inability to sleep at all, is of course a serious physical issue and may require healing work or medication. If we are possessed with a desire to sleep other than at normal proscribed times, it may be that we need to take a closer look at our situations and undertakings. If we are permanently stressed to the point where sleep evades us, we should see this for what it is—a warning that we need to look more deeply at our life choices and general situation.

Keywords Upright: Cessation of activity. Rest. Repose. Refreshment. Refuelling. Reappraisal. Nighttime understanding.

Keywords Reversed: Too much sleep. Craving cessation. Lacking refreshment. Troubled sleep. Lack of sleep.

21: THE DREAMER

The Dreamer follows The Sleeper here and is obviously closely connected— but dreams do not always follow sleep, and when they do, they may drive us away from the realisations we require from our time in restful oblivion. Throughout much of the ancient world, dream interpretation was considered one of the most important means of divination. The Celts and others practiced a form of incubation, where a dream state was induced by placing the sleeper into a completely lightless environment and later in waking him or her with bright light. This triggered a visionary state and enabled the sleeper to capture the hidden meanings in their dream imagery. In ancient Egypt, dreams were considered extremely important. A dream book dating from the reign of Ramesses II (1279–1213 BCE) lists different kinds of dreams, including those that prophesied bad things, which were written in red. In ancient Hawaii, dreams were analysed to help important decisions. The word for dream, *moe'uhane*, means "soul sleep," and the Hawaiians believed that their souls communed with those of their ancestors during sleep. No two types of dream interpretation are the same. In Islam, for example, dreams are given a great deal of importance, and there are said to be three kinds of dreams: true dreams, in which visions are imparted; dreams in which you speak to yourself and learn things you already knew; and the bad dreams that originate with the devil. Other cultures remind us that all life was dreamed into being by the Creator, thus emphasising the importance of dreams to enable creativity. Here this is the central feature of this card. The Dreamer seeks knowledge and wisdom though sleep, actively encountering and interpreting the images that filter through to them. In a reading, it points to the importance of acknowledging the value of our dreams and learning the truths they carry. It also indicates a need to take a different perspective than the everyday, automatic response that we are used to. Dreams offer insights we should not ignore. The same is true of the ancient technique known as "daydreaming," in which we often drift away and return with clearer understanding than those we began with.

Reversed, we may give too much unthinking importance to our dreams. Interpretation does not mean accepting the first, most obvious ideas that swim to the surface as we awaken. We should also be aware of false dreams, where we actively seek to bend the meaning to our own ends. We should not forget the character of Morpheus and his brothers in Greek and Roman tradition (see card 20: The Sleep), who are given to taking on forms that are sought after by the dreamer to lead them astray by offering them enticements that work against their true understanding.

Keywords Upright: Dreams. Other perspectives. Daydreaming. Insight. Visions. Creative intuition.

Keywords Reversed: False dreams. Nightmares. Unthinking interpretation. Misleading images.

22: STRENGTH

Strength, also known as Fortitude, originally referenced the figure of the Greek hero Hercules, struggling with the Nemean lion, one of his twelve mighty labors that have been identified with the signs of the zodiac. Later, this figure morphed into a female aspect, perhaps the nymph Cyrene, who was observed wrestling with a lion by Apollo, who took a shine to her as a result. Some have seen this as the taming of male energies by the feminine, or of the dark rage of the unconscious mind by the clearer element of conscious intention. But the strength acknowledged by the imagery is not just that of the physical realm. It represents strength of feeling, strength of character—even, possibly, moral strength. Strength represents the ability to keep going in the face of adversity, and as such it has been described as the warrior card, but this is to limit it. Strength of will also transcends the bounds of human ability, and all the countless tales of heroic achievement (not always in warfare but equally in exploration, sport, and creativity) are very much a part of this card's meaning. In readings it signifies the eagerness of the seeker to attack the problem, and indicates a strong resource of strength across the board. Above all, the calmness and self-possession of the figure depicted here points to the use of strength in the face of adversity. Anger is seldom a good response to anything; calmness shows how you may deal with whatever issue you face without becoming overwhelmed. You may be required to tame the forces within you that seek to meet every opposition in a combative way. Strength held in check remains a reserve that you can tap into; it does not require you to attack every problem at full stretch. Sometimes you may need to turn to a powerful friend or guide who helps usher in the moment of truth, which must be faced without fear.

Reversed, you may find yourself prey to weakness, an inability to grasp the situation or to find the energy necessary to combat a testing issue. Beyond this, it is about an inability to master one's fears or to combat the powerful urge to fight your way through a seemingly impenetrable situation. Be careful not to abuse your power and let impatience overwhelm your more reasoned impulses.

Keywords Upright: Strength. Force. Courage. Power. Ability. Authority. Commanding presence. Inner resources. Endurance. Fortitude. Calming the situation.

Keywords Reversed: Weakness. Sickness. Tyranny. Abuse of power. Indifference. Anger. Impatience.

23: THE FISHERMAN

The Fisherman has a curious history of interpretation, from the words of Jesus to his disciples—"I will make you fishers of men"—to the character known as the Rich Fisherman in the Grail story. Even the great psychoanalyst Carl Jung, used the metaphor of a man fishing whose line connected with another man fishing below the water and so on, taking the idea deeper and deeper into the subconscious landscape of the mind. The Rich Fisherman is another name for the Wounded King in the Grail myth. He is one of the guardians of the sacred vessel who is wounded in both thighs (usually interpreted to refer to the generative organs) and unable to be healed until the Grail winner uses the same spear that caused the wound to heal him. This is a theme that goes very deep into the human psyche—wounds that can be healed only by reversing their original cause. In *The Fool's New Journey Tarot*, it stands for a number of things: the quest for healing, the ability to trawl for memories and truths, filling our nets with the treasures of the soul, and catching the answers you need to solve the issues you bring to the cards. It is also about taking a chance, casting your nets upon the waters until they capture something of value to you alone. You are the fisherman of your own fate.

Reversed, the card can suggest you are given to taking risks, expecting your nets or fishing line to bring to the surface everything and anything you want. Be careful of relying too much upon others, or on your feeling that nothing can go wrong. Throwing caution to the winds can be a dangerous approach to any issue—if you are determined to do so, try to prepare for the possibility of failure.

Keywords Upright: Catching what you need. Taking a chance/punt. A gamble. Risk. Providing for your needs. The search for healing. Trawling for memory.

Keywords Reversed: Overconfidence. Too great a degree of self-belief. Taking a risk. Throwing caution to the winds.

24: THE TEACHER

The Teacher is one who holds the keys to learning and wisdom, who extends the invitation to learn, to grow, and to prosper by expanding your horizons and seeking out paths that you might otherwise not see or wish to follow. It can be someone whose teachings you wish to follow, often a charismatic leader who proffers words and ideas that speak to you. It can also be you yourself, if you are devoted to sharing your own learning with others. It signifies the opening up of wisdom (and as such is paired with Wisdom in the sequence of *The Fool's New Journey*) and its promulgation by an individual. It is also, at a deeper level, about the natural inclination to learn, which is in everyone. If you feel that this is being smothered by others, you should be ready to check for any signs of a lessening of your abilities. Your innate ability to teach yourself, to learn by your mistakes, is all part of the meaning of this card. In a reading it may refer to things preventing you from sharing your knowledge or skill, or a failure among others to pass on their own significant wisdom. You may be aware of yourself as a pathmaker, or a guide to others, or as an exemplar of wisdom and truth.

Reversed, the indication is that you need to be careful that what you are offering is truly of benefit to others. It is all too easy to become an expert and an influencer, but if you fail to take the time to learn and grow yourself, how can you pass along your skills to others? You would not set yourself up as a plumber or electrician after one lesson or reading a basic book on the subject. You may need to look *for* a teacher in whichever area calls out to you, and give time to fulfill your own journey until you are in a position to teach others.

Keywords Upright: Education and learning. Pathmaking. Sharing wisdom. Advice. Guidance. Support. Exemplar.

Keywords Reversed: Egotistical belief in your own teaching skills. Leading others astray. Sharing uncertain truths. Failing to see the way forward. Bad examples.

25: THE WORKER

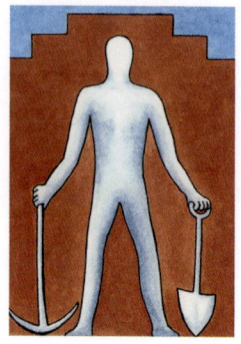

The Worker has not always had a good reputation. Road builders, those doing the washing up in a restaurant, decorators, and, before them, servants and, earlier still, pages (who still feature in classic decks) and of course slaves—these and many more have been branded as menial. But without those who do the work, the world grinds to a halt. Life itself is threatened. Often we do not stop to think that we are workers too—maybe we have what is called a profession rather than a job, but we are still workers. An emigrant fleeing the Nazi regime in World War II said that for him, providing the work was honourable, it did not matter whether it was in areas considered superior or those perceived as menial. Within *The Fool's New Journey* sequence, The Worker stands for things that concern us much of the time: the necessity most of us have for employment—not just to live but also to fill our days with the satisfaction of doing a job and doing it well. Writers, artists, composers, and musicians may not be thought of as workers, but if work is carrying out a task to the best of their abilities, then they are very much so. The Worker knows his or her craft and applies their skills to whatever work is required. He or she knows that the task is an honourable one—provided, of course, that they are working for an ethically sound organization or running their own business ethically. They offer a service freely and, it is hoped, with joy. In a reading the card represents every one of us, and as such it is influential in any enquiry or issue raised. Any kind of work is covered by this, and though we have portrayed a very basic figure of the worker, sitting behind a desk or digging a hole in the earth are equally relevant in any reading where this card appears.

Reversed, we see those who seek to avoid work or do slapdash and unsatisfactory jobs that can threaten the safety of those they work for. Also, the satisfaction of work well done tends to flow backward, leading to feelings of disaffection, aggression, and envy. These may be people for whom the ethics and honesty of employment may be darker and more manipulative.

Keywords Upright: Earning a living. Knowing your craft or skill. Offering a service. Job of work. Employment. Job satisfaction.

Keywords Reversed: Dissatisfaction. Anger. Slapdash work. Reluctance to seek employment. Failure to do a good job. Manipulation.

26: WHEEL OF FORTUNE

The Wheel dominated the writings of medieval and Renaissance philosophers. Everywhere they looked in the world, they saw manifestations of this image in the lives and deaths of great men and women, who rose to the top of the wheel and just as rapidly fell as it turned. Fortuna herself (Dame Fortune), who oversaw The Wheel, is one of the most powerful deities of the ancient world, and there is evidence to suggest that her influence continued long after the coming of Christianity. One of the great books of the Middle Ages, *The Consolation of Philosophy* by Boethius, tells how he was wrongly imprisoned and kept up his spirits by dialoguing with the great female figure of Philosophy, who appears to him in his cell. She instructs him in the power of her cousin Dame Fortune, whose wheel can upset anyone from commoner to king as she turns it, gifting them with good or bad fortune according to her whim. What we mean by fortune—whether good or bad—varies enormously according to how we live and see life. For some, luck is everything—they see events going well, or ill, and pronounce them to be governed by luck. For others, fortune is something to be worked for, to seek with every ounce of diligence. In reality, fortune is something over which (or whom) we have little control. It may represent something good coming our way, better prospects and greater income, but it can just as easily be the opposite (irrespective of whether the card is upright or not).

Reversed, in most readings the presence of this card can upset the outcome of the answer offered. Essentially, we make our own luck. Because of this, the normal rules about reversed cards are less effective. What appears to be a negative response may turn out to be something else entirely, and even though the card may represent a reversal of fortune, only the placing of other cards in the reading will define whether this is a good or bad thing. Fortune can deal us many different kinds of fate, and whatever comes, we have to deal with it appropriately. Above all it represents change, whether for the better or worse, depending entirely on the circumstances.

Keywords Upright: Lucky and unlucky change. Peace. Shifting viewpoint. Success/unsuccess. Destiny. Fortune good and bad. Inevitability.

Keywords Reversed: Bad luck. Failure. Reversal of fortunes. Unexpected events. Progress. Beginnings and endings.

27: CHAOS

Chaos is something we are all, in one way or another, familiar with. In Greek myth, Eris was the goddess of chaos, strife, and discord. Some accounts say she was the daughter of Zeus and Hera along with her sister Harmonia. Others told that she was the daughter of Nyx (darkness and night). In Roman tradition, Discordia and Concordia held the natural chaos of the universe in balance. These myths tell us a lot about the way Chaos works. At ground level it can be anything between a chaotic style of living; balancing a job, children, pets, and household tasks on a long day and under difficult circumstances; and a larger degree of chaotic thought or action. Chaos can be seen to operate outside the home and the personal in the often-chaotic world in which we live. And the association with darkness and night (sometimes nothingness) tells us that chaos is both a natural phenomenon and something to be wary of. The English word "chaos" is associated with the ancient Greek word meaning "abyss." At this time, Chaos was believed to be the emptiness that existed before the cosmos came into being, while later it became associated with Tartarus, the lower world into which spirits fell. In time, this morphed into the proposal of chaos theory, an interdisciplinary scientific idea coupled with a branch of mathematics that focuses on the patterns inherent in everything. It seeks to find order within chaos itself, and this is the principle on which this card works. No matter how chaotic our thoughts, our feelings, or our actions may seem, there is a degree of organisation that subsumes all of these into a place of stillness. Curiously, chaos is predictable, though the effect is so complex that it takes a mathematician of genius to work it out! The most famous example is the butterfly effect, which says that if a butterfly flaps its wings in one place, it will ultimately cause a hurricane thousands of miles and ages away in an unknown future. So many other influences occur between one action and its cause that we cannot see it—but predictability is a part of this. We may not be able to track the millions of tiny events that bring about a single happening in our lives, but they are there anyway. Not everything is predicable or viewable, but the patterns are important whether we acknowledge them or not. In a reading, this card is therefore very much about seeking (and finding) order in the chaos that affects us. Look to the cards on either side for clarity here, or simply allow the idea of a peaceful centre to fill your thoughts.

Reversed, the picture is less happy. It is all about the kind of uncontrolled chaos that we ourselves bring about in our lives, spreading ourselves too thinly and trying to master several disciplines at once. This creates a storm of chaotic actions and thoughts, in which it is far too easy to lose our sense of purpose or direction. Any thoughts of order will fly before you and requires careful contemplation to bring yourself back from the edge. Meditation may help with this, in helping you to locate the causes of the destructive whirlwind and try to find the point of stillness at its centre.

Keywords Upright: Chaotic living. Seeking cause and effect. Finding the point of stillness at the centre of the storm. Predicting the causes of chaos. Chaos theory. Collecting the shards of life and restoring them.

Keywords Reversed: Fragmentation. Things out of kilter. Feeling confused. Breakdown of the normal. Losing direction. Doing too much.

28: DEATH

Death is, understandably perhaps, one of the most feared cards to appear in any deck. Despite the fact that it represents much more than physical death, it can change, block, or divide aspects of a reading. The presence of the grim skeleton, often with a scythe, which he wields to fell the living, has cast his long shadow over the Western world from earliest times. But in many early representations, Death's scythe is used not only to cut bodies into pieces but also to cut away weeds that strangle our growth. In the oldest texts relating to the theme, especially the medieval mystery plays, Death addresses everyone as equals. There is no escaping him, and no matter how powerful you are, he will catch up with you in the end. This is often treated as a grim comedy, suggesting that we should laugh in the face of death whenever possible. Many of the greatest stories written in the Middle Ages and after are about characters such as Faust who find ways to trick death, or to extend their lives beyond a normal span. Our image shows Death as a top-hatted skeleton raising his hat politely to those he encounters. He's not friendly, exactly, but represents the comedic aspects of so many of the ideas associated with him. In addition, three birds fly overhead, souls on their journey home or doves of peace, which relate this card to The Wasteland card.

The card is a formidable one, as we would expect. Many readers shy away from its appearance in a reading simply because of an innate fear. However, as most readers will tell you, death in this instance rarely means physical death, but more often the death of an old idea or way of living, cutting oneself adrift from the stream of things and finding a new way of being. It can also suggest the relief one feels at the ending of a protracted struggle—whether with illness or any trenchant problem—and as such often indicates this in a reading. It encourages change of the most positive kind—leaving behind old, stale, worn-out ways, changing your job, school, or relationship—always moving toward a positive outcome. It can also mean disillusionment, an awakening to the recognition that one's life needs to change. This is an aspect of Death in which he is welcomed as an old friend.

Reversed, the opposite is true. It refers to stagnation, immobility, the inability to accept the need for change or to implement any break with old ways. You may be dealing with inertia, the simple weight of circumstances rolling over you. The best-laid plans may go astray, but the position and relationship of other cards in the reading should be considered.

Keywords Upright: Change. Renewal. Transformation. New direction. Rebirth. Mortality. Disillusionment. Separation. Ending. Inevitability.

Keywords Reversed: Stagnation. Immobility. Inertia. Discouragement. Failure of plans to manifest.

29: THE SORROWFUL

The Sorrowful are those who, for whatever reason, feel their lives filled with nothing but sorrow. They are those who have lost, have found themselves wandering without form in their lives, or have no room for joy or motion, whose emotions have overwhelmed them and left them desolate upon a lonely shore. No longer free to see any joy around them, they continue to suffer until Hope or balance are restored to them (see card 34: Hope). In Greek myth the sorrowful ones were represented by the Algea, spirits representing pain, suffering, grief, and distress. All brought sadness and tears in their wake. Less extreme was the goddess Oizys, who represented misery and sadness, as well as anxiety, grief, depression, and misfortune. Indeed, her Roman name, Miseria, gave us the English word "misery," while her brother, Penthos, was the god of mourning and lamentation. In a reading, this card can represent both the enquirer or someone for whom they are reading. Usually it is a person who has suffered great loss and cannot come to terms with life. They may also be characters in the theatre of living, who wear the mask of Sorrow but do not fully understand the true meaning of sadness. They are cousins to The Merry (card 37), who sometimes stretch themselves too far in their quest for happiness. Both the images here are based on the idea of ancient theatrical masks worn to express emotion that could be seen from the farthest position in the auditorium and that also showed that they could be removed or even swapped for other responses to events. Above all, it is important to understand that this is not an utterly negative card. Sorrow is a natural and normal response to events, whether the death of a loved one or the loss of a belief or direction that seems no longer to answer our need.

Reversed, we are reminded that like all of the traditionally darker cards in the Tarot (Death, The Tower, The Hanged Man), these are not irreversible but can, indeed, be brought to bear in our issues and help us find our way to a place of acceptance and resolution. Also that they do not always represent the worst that can happen—Death rarely means physical death, The Hanged Man offers himself to be hanged upside down in order to learn greater wisdom, and The Tower is more about a break with old ways than a literal breaking down of life. Thus, while the reversal of Sorrow does not necessarily mean happiness, it promises the possibility that we may find a way to accept the darkest of situations and become aware of a more hopeful future.

Keywords Upright: Sorrow. Grief. Bereavement. Depression. Contemplating sadness. Natural sorrow. Tragedy.

Keywords Reversed: Seeking and finding a cure for sorrow. Enjoying life again. Restoration after a long period of sorrow. Awakening.

30: THE TOWER

The Tower, also known as The Thunderbolt, The Lightning-Struck Tower, The House of God, or The Hospital, is one of the oldest and most consistently reproduced images in Tarot. The origins of the image go back to the Middle Ages, where there are numerous references to towers broken down by God's lightning, sometimes followed by scenes depicting the expulsion of human beings from the paradisal realm of Eden. It also reflects the fascination of the medieval world with the story of the Tower of Babel, which became a symbol of the desire of powerful rulers to control more of the world around them, and reminded them of the results of pride and hubris. Here we have referenced one of the darkest moments in recent history—the attack on the Twin Towers in New York City in 2001. The sense is of an abrupt and catastrophic moment of change, which is often the basic understanding of the card. But we should seek to look beyond this to the secondary meanings, which include the breaking down of old and outworn structures. This may seem unsettling but can refer to the restoration and restructuring of things in a more potent manner. It is important that we do not always assume the worst, in a Tarot reading or in any part of life, but seek, rather, to see beyond the immediate, darker events to a place where calmer waters await us. Some of the earliest references to this card refer to The Tower as belonging to The Devil (see card 32), so that the breaking of The Tower is actually the destruction of evil rather than good, and thus is it interpreted in more recent decks. Seen from this viewpoint, the divinatory meaning is more positive. Sometimes we must face painful and seemingly destructive events in order for the path to be cleared and old, no-longer-required aspects of our lives broken down in order to allow fresh growth. The other ancient title for this card, The Hospital, makes this even clearer: a hospital can indeed be seen as a fearful place, yet it is also a place where healing can and does result.

Reversed, the immediate response to drawing this card may well be one of despair. Unforeseen events, loss, denial, and obstacles that we have to face may seem overwhelming, but it is important to remember that change is not always a bad thing, and that the lightning strike may represent a flash of insight or inspiration that can lead to a reassessment of your life path, beliefs, or intentions, as well as a painful readjustment or something that requires confrontation before peace can result. Also a sense of just atonement. Though it is not seen as reversing the inherent meaning, it gives us room to consider that even the darkest meaning can be overturned if we seek out its hidden side.

Keywords Upright: Sudden and shocking change. The breaking down of old structures. Clearing the path. Cleansing energy. Reassessment. Catharsis. Hubris. Reversal. Calamity.

Keywords Reversed: Denial. Failings. Poverty. Unforeseen events. Catastrophe. Loss. Cataclysm. An obstacle to be faced. Seeking light in the darkest moments.

31: THE DOWNFALL

The Downfall is about falling from grace, losing one's reputation, being demoted and sometimes thrown out of one's established position in life. Typically it concerns someone who has risen to the heights in their profession and has become hugely popular and fated by all, who suddenly, and often unexpectedly, becomes reviled, cast out, accused of all kinds of unsavory practices or unacceptable behaviour. This does not mean that the person or persons concerned are guilty of any of the things of which they are accused; they may be the victims of gossip, deliberate attacks, or misrepresentation. The image here recalls the Christian myth of Lucifer, once the Morning Star and Lightbringer, cast out of Heaven for rebelling against God and subsequently reviled and assumed to be the fount of all evil (see card 32: The Devil) Whether one ascribes to this or not as a matter of personal belief, arguments can be made that suggest that the fallen angel appeared because of the belief that evil, as the opposite of goodness, therefore required a figurehead, just as the more ancient beliefs had their own dark and troublesome gods, such as Pluto in Greek mythology; Loki in Norse mythology; Loviatar, the Finnish goddess of pain and death; Apophis, the god of chaos in ancient Egypt; and Lamashtu in the Mesopotamian pantheon. Lucifer seems to have been chosen because he came to represent pride, hubris even, within the theology of early Christianity. In terms of human life, individuals can also become polarised as reflections of negative or unethical behaviour—sometimes with unquestionable accuracy, at other times brought about through personal animosity. The card therefore reflects the uncertainty and sometimes unfairness of such occurrences and asks that we look beyond the surface of accusatory language to the possibility of other truths. This refers both to outside figures, such as work colleagues, people to whom we have always turned for probity, and to our own lives and actions. We may think of ourselves as honest and upright members of society, but we sometimes have to face the reality that we might be acting out of self-interest. In matters of the heart, we may find ourselves falling out of love or being cast aside without good reason. Here too we must search our consciences to be sure we have not erred ourselves.

Reversed, the card is about the restoration of a lost reputation, of standing up for ourselves and offering proof of our honest and ethical behaviour. This can often be a long and difficult process, without guarantees that we will prove ourselves innocent of what we may have been accused, but the essence of it is to hold fast to the knowledge that we are who we say we are, and that the accusations of others may be prompted by jealousy, self-serving, and beliefs contrary to our own. It offers the hope of being once again acknowledged, loved, and recognised for our true selves, and of rising once more to the position in society or personal life from which we fell.

Keywords Upright: Falling from grace. Demotion. Falling out of favour or popularity. Overthrow. Loss of reputation. Falling out of love.

Keywords Reversed: Rising. Reestabilishing oneself. Acknowledged. Recognised. Reputation restored. Love returning.

32: THE DEVIL

The Devil has nearly always been represented as a monstrous, deformed creature with bat wings, horns, cloven hoofs, etc. Rather as the Christian Church used the figure of the fallen angel Lucifer as a peg on which to hang every possible manifestation of evil (see card 31: The Downfall), so in Tarot the stories of demons stealing men's souls, and images of the damned, shuffling their way toward the gaping mouth of Hell, would have been present in most churches. Before The Devil ousted all earlier creatures, the image was probably a representation of Typhon, the dragon-monster of classical myth who emerged from the underworld brandishing a flaming torch and bringing disaster in his wake. More recently, following the esoteric revival of the 19th century and the blossoming of pagan beliefs in our own time, The Devil has become identified with the god Pan, spirit or nature, and abandonment and, as such, deemed a positive influence. Despite this, the essential meaning has not changed. In whatever form he comes, The Devil brings connotations of self-aggrandizement or, if we think of him in terms of magic, as the "black" magician, whose aim is only to raise power for himself rather than the "white" magician, who seeks to raise power to help others. Here, we have shown him holding a cup in which he offers the drink of selfishness. The central meaning of the card revolves around deceit, lies, and trickery—all aspects of "devilish" influence. Almost always it represents either the reader or someone close to him or her, someone who is self-serving and will do anything to get their own way, to rise to the top of the heap, to be important. It is the fantasy of childhood self-aggrandizement transferred to the adult, and it can be very destructive. If it represents you, it indicates that you like to break the rules, to act selfishly to fulfill your own desires, irrespective of how this may affect others. Essentially it is about fear and self-love, which in general terms means that whoever feels this is unable to relate properly to anyone else. Some will feel that they are too perfect to ever find anyone who can reach their impossibly high standards; others are simply afraid to acknowledge that anything or anyone matters beyond themselves—or, in a more extreme form, that everyone is out to get them. It is all too easy to become trapped in this kind of narrow self-delusional approach, which sooner or later leads to the poisoning of life itself. It could indeed be said that the card suggests a harsh journey to reach reality, where the delusions fall away and individuals see themselves and their lives as they really are.

Reversed, the card indicates an effort to throw off negative concepts and to grow again in a more positive way, essentially to free oneself from enslavement to the ego. It suggests optimism rather than the bleak selfishness of the upright card, and just as the devil-may-care, cavalier behaviour of the person represented by the card, here the reader cares for others and seeks to find value in life though helping those less fortunate than himself, or herself.

Keywords Upright: Self-aggrandizement. Power out of control. Passion. Lust. Malevolence. Self-destruction. Subservience violence. Unprincipled behavior. Psychosis. Knowing better than others. Nonconsensual. Bitterness. Anger. Obsession.

Keywords Reversed: Release from slavery. Optimism. Concern for others. Awakening to the value of the self. Virtue. Morality.

33: THE QUESTIONER

The Questioner represents those who question everything. There are many reasons why they choose to do this. Curiosity is one—the desire to know and understand the world in which they live and the worlds beyond the physical. Many will be prompted by the uncertainty they feel about their lives and those who surround them. They may feel threatened by things, people, creatures, or events and spend much of their time seeking answers. This may lead to overdependence upon knowing every small detail. If they are about to set out on a journey, they will check the route twenty times and make certain that the tank is full of petrol more than once (assuming they are driving, or that the bus/train/aircraft/ship is running on time and that there are no likely blockages on the way. If they are contemplating a move from one job to another, they will list the pros and cons and then relist them several times, checking everything and even looking to find out about future colleagues. All of this may seem far too much and generally unhealthful, but much depends on the spirit in which it is carried out. Groups of questioners will ask countless questions until answers are forthcoming. Individuals will challenge decisions made at every level, from basic workplace to government department. Some will see them as a nuisance, but often they will find a way that transcends their annoyance and brings genuine enlightenment. Those of us who question the Tarot are questioners, at whatever level we seek to know more. Scientists and philosophers have asked questions for centuries and have led us though clouds of ignorance toward understanding. To ask a question, or as many as are needed, is an import action. Sometimes we need to keep asking until we get the answer we need. Otherwise we drift through life accepting the reality that we see. In a time when "fake news" and the misrepresentation of truth are widespread, we need Questioners to look as closely as possible at any situation. In a reading this may show us the need to question a decision, or to point to someone who is already asking to understand the issue we are hoping to solve.

Reversed, this points to a situation, person, or group going nowhere. They will sit on the fence staring at the world around them and seeing almost nothing. They may seem certain of their approach to a given situation, but in reality they are almost certainly following a pattern designed in an earlier time. They will not ask questions or seek to understand alternative views. They are so determined and blind to fresh thinking that they will never ask the questions that need to be asked. They may seem bold, but often they are hiding behind a received and unquestioned set of rules.

Keywords Upright: Curiosity. Questioning everything. Caution. Uncertainty. Seeking solutions. Searching for the truth. The seeker.

Keywords Reversed: Certainty. Determination. Looking but not seeing. Hidebound. Stuck in a rut. Afraid to ask questions

34: HOPE

Hope is something we all need. In our darkest moments we hope to find a solution, an escape, or help of whatever kind is available to bring us back from the edge. In ancient traditions the goddesses of Hope were the most often supplicated. In the Greek pantheon, Elpis was the spirit of Hope. In Rome, Spes. In the Hellenic tale of Pandora's jar, we learn that when Prometheus stole the gift of fire from heaven, Zeus, enraged, trapped all the evils that brought sorrow to mankind—including sickness, death, and fear—in a jar, which he gave to Pandora, the first woman, to keep. But Pandora became curious to know what was within the jar, and opened it. At once, all the evils flew out and spiralled back up to Olympus—all but one: Elpis. Hope remained behind to offer comfort to mankind. She is usually portrayed, as here, as a young woman carrying a bunch of flowers, symbols of the promise she brings. The Greek philosopher Hesiod wrote: "As long as man lives and sees the light of the sun, let him show piety to the gods and count on Elpis. Let him pray to the gods . . . sacrificing to Elpis first and last." In a reading, Hope can turn aside the darkness and show the way to discover healing and joy in the face of adversity. She brings a positive breath of fresh air to any situation and supports us in our search for answers and help. Above all, Hope offers us balance and truth and opens the way forward. She is one of the best-aspected cards in the deck and should always be recognised as having a powerful influence upon the whole reading.

Reversed, Hope turns dark and casts a shadow over the hopeful outcome we are seeking. This does not mean that we should give up. Even with her face turned away from us, the presence of Hope is still powerful and essentially positive despite everything. As with all Tarot readings, consider the cards that have fallen on either side of Hope. How do these modify or reverse the reversal?

Keywords Upright: Hopefulness. Comfort. Belief that all will be well. Support. Balance. Clear sight. Respect for all. Watchfulness. Protection. Calmer waters.

Keywords Reversed: Strife. Fear. Hopelessness. Sense of danger. Loss of direction.

35: FORGETTING

Forgetting is about the things we allow ourselves to forget through lack of attention, deliberate avoidance, or loss of mental acuity. We can lose so much in this way, sometimes by letting things go that we might need, at other times when we no longer see the importance of memory. We may find that inspiration deserts us, as the remembrance of ideas and dreams vanishes into a fog of forgetting. The bird of thought flies away in this image, especially if we fail to attend to it. We should keep our memories fresh and sharp. As the poet W. B. Yeats wrote, "Forgetting and remembering, we lay waste our dreams." This is a reference to the way memories so easily melt way or become confused. Sometimes we depend upon memories too much, especially when we misremember the true nature of events in the past. In a reading, this says that we need to revisit our lost memories, bringing them back into focus and ensuring that we do not repeat patterns that fail to aid us in our understanding of the patterns in our lives. It also refers to those who have been, and are, forgotten. How easy it is to allow our memories of those who are no longer present, or have moved, to melt away. Our friendships and memories of those who have passed are every bit as important now as they were, and should never be neglected. Likewise, those who have simply left our personal sphere should be remembered and links reestablished when possible.

Reversed, the card suggests we are overwhelmed with memories, sometimes a cause of pain or fear. We should not forget that there are times when forgetfulness is a blessing. If we cannot let traumatic things fall into forgetfulness, then we may be in a constant state of flight or fight, forever trying to let go, reliving the trauma over and over. This condition seals us into reliving fear or terror. A need for therapy may be indicated here.

Keywords Upright: Lack of attention. Avoidance. Loss of mental acuity. Forgetfulness. Lack of imagination.

Keywords Reversed: Recovering painful memories. Fears returning. Trauma. A need for release.

36: REMEMBERING

Remembering is about recalling things we have forgotten, and is linked with the previous card, Forgetting. It is about finding or rediscovering inspiration, putting together fragments of memory, feeling, or thought to uncover or re-create something new. The bird of fire in the picture is Thought itself, finding its way back to us after a period of forgetting, drawing us up into the world of memory and helping us reassemble broken memories to form patterns we recognise. We are, when all is said and done, the sum of our memories. Everything we recollect, from childhood to the present, from dreams, thoughts, ideas, and inspiration, are all things we need to remember—just as we remember birthdays, addresses, or where we left our keys. Reassembling memories is as important as recalling the germ of an idea that we may choose to develop into something greater. In classical mythology, Mnemosyne, the goddess of memory, is the child of Uranus (Heaven) and Gaea (Earth), the primal deities of creation, showing that memory is one of the most important aspects of human life. She later gives birth to the Nine Muses, fathered by Zeus. These nine are the foundation of all creative activity, and as children of Memory they demonstrate the importance of their mother's influence over humankind. Our very identity emerges from this. In a reading, the card may signify the importance of remembering fragments of thought and activity. If you are about to undertake a new project, remember to give attention to things you may think you have forgotten. Just as you might lose your way on a road you have not travelled for a long time, now, by recovering your memory of the route, opportunities are opened up around you. The celebration of memory is often triggered by attending a memorable event, such as a birth or a funeral. In both instances the memory of these things is important: on the one hand, to remember the person who is no longer present, and on the other hand, to establish a first set of memories of the newly born infant. These are the things we need to recall when we embark on a new phase of life, either at a beginning or an end. Remembering those who are no longer with us in this life does not just refer to immediate relatives or friends, but also more distant ancestors—known or unknown. Remembering them can bring great joy and benefit to us—their wisdom still remains, and we can learn much from it.

Reversed, the story reflects a catastrophic loss of acuity, of fearing to remember things that happened in the past and that you do not want to be part of your life. Traumatic events, often in childhood, may surface suddenly and block the way for you. Here, you may *need* to forget, to see the dark dreams of the past as having no power over you. Let those memories go and look elsewhere for inspiration.

Keywords Upright: Recalling. Reinspired. Reimagination. Reenvisaging. Remembering. Memorial. Restoring what is broken. Making sense of the past. Ancestral wisdom.

Keywords Reversed: Lost sense of identity. Loss of inspiration. Fearful memories. Releasing old patterns and finding new. Forgetting the ancestors.

37: THE MERRY

The Merry are cousins to The Sorrowful, those who are, or who seem to be, entirely happy with whatever life brings them—every glass seen to be half full (or perhaps half empty!). They see harmony where others see chaos, they are friendly toward everyone, and they enjoy their daily interaction with living, in spite of anything that may occur. Sometimes this can be entirely brought about by an inability to read the truth of a situation, to be blind to the pitfalls and traps that may lie ahead of them as they journey through life. It can be seen as thoughtless and even selfish behaviour and recalls those to whom life can appear overwhelmingly full of joy and delight. But this can be a hollow way of living—and can mean that the person who seems eternally optimistic is in fact hiding from reality. The distance between The Merry and The Sorrowful is less than a heartbeat of time or a thin line drawn into the dust, and the card may point to this in a reading. It also tells us that we may be in danger of becoming lost in the world of merriment. As with all manifest points of view, we may find ourselves without the ability to recognise the reality of a situation.

Reversed, the card veers more toward places where The Sorrowful dwell. It shows how easily the scales can unbalance and fall from our eyes, leaving us prey to dark thoughts and feelings of being forgotten or cast out. Sadness and emotional breakdown can quickly replace jollity and merriment, leaving us uncertain how to behave or what steps to take. As with all such extreme moods, it requires the balance of opposites, the tempering of extreme happiness with at least the acknowledgment that other states may exist. In a reading it usually points to such a need, which may cut across all areas of life.

Keywords Upright: Joyful. Enjoyment. Embodying joy. Carefree. Laughing at life. Putting on the mask.

Keywords Reversed: Sadness. Careworn. Emotionally overwhelmed. Needing restoration. Feeling forgotten.

38: TEMPERANCE

Temperance, once listed among the Cardinal Virtues, is perhaps the least well understood in our time because of its association with refraining from alcohol or excess. In reality, temperance means a great deal more than this, being more concerned with a balanced outlook on life and a restrained way of temperate living. The origin of the word is the Latin *temperare,* meaning "to exchange" or "to mingle." Hence the traditional Tarot image is of a woman (or an angel) pouring liquid from one vessel to another, and we have chosen to keep this imagery here. This is often presumed to mean that she was adding water to wine—a means of being more temperate. In fact, it has more to do with the exchange of the liquid contained in the vessels, a mingling of two streams of energy, or even of past and future influences, which provide greater balance. Some commentators have suggested that the figure was once Ganymede, the cup bearer of Zeus, but most Tarots portray her as female, so that she is more likely to be Iris, a nymph who journeyed to the river Styx to fill her cup with water. This signified a visit to the land of the dead, of forgetting, to visit which and to return was indicative of renewed life. Temperance thus represents the balanced view that life is capable of renewal in even the darkest circumstances.

The interpretation of the card is all about moderating your behavior, living your life temperately, balancing the past and future streams of activity, and learning to approach problems with due care and attention rather than rushing in and meeting every challenge aggressively. Imbalances in the body create the right conditions for illness and disease to flourish, so that living a balanced lifestyle is all important. In a reading, the card may indicate that you need to address this aspect of your life, or to confirm that you are already living in harmony with yourself and the universe. It also points to the wisdom of keeping things moving, of allowing a good exchange of ideas and feelings in any situation—whether work or love related. This should not, however, be confused with a need to be in perpetual motion, to act impulsively; rather, it shows that sometimes it is best to do nothing, to allow the problem to work itself out.

Reversed, the implication is one of an intemperate attitude toward everything, a sense that life easily gets on top of us, driving us to increasingly furious responses where a more measured approach would be more helpful. To ignore this could result in quarrels, clashes of will, and an increasingly fragmented life, which can lead to illness. To be governed by an aggressive temperament is hardly welcome in most roles, both personal and work oriented. The truth is simply that balance is all important, and that keeping a foot very firmly in both camps can be a lot more productive than throwing in your lot with one side or another.

Keywords Upright: Balance. Patience. Calmness. Moderation. Adaptability. Frugality. Serenity. Harmony. Self-control. Mingling of past and future. Merging. Synthesis. Good boundaries. Moderation.

Keywords Reversed: Discord. Conflict of interest. Hostility. Frustration. Competitiveness. Impatience. Aggressive attitude. Illness.

39: THE DIVINER

The Diviner is one who has the skill to use whatever gift of seership and vision comes along. She or he may use the Tarot, consult oracles, or gaze into a mirror or a pool of water in order to discover truths. They are likely to be people who already possess such abilities, and who, when they look at a question, consider a situation, or fathom a difficult set of circumstances, are likely to see the truth that underlies it in an inspired moment. Most solutions uncovered this way show that both the seeker and that which is sought are connected, and that the enquirer may possess a gift for understanding patterns, whether in the stars, in the grains of sand, or as ripples in the water. Nostradamus (1503–1566), one of the greatest diviners and seers of all time, described his own favoured method of seeing, sometimes called scrying. Sitting alone in his study, lit only by a flickering candle, bent over a bowl of water, to which he sometimes added pungent oils, he writes how "*I emptied my soul, brain, and heart of all care and attained a state of tranquility and stillness of mind, which are prerequisites for predicting.*" Other kinds of divination exist: divining for water, blind springs, energy lines in the landscape, and the location of powerful places in the world. These gifts too are part of the inner life of the diviner, who feels, with their innermost being, things normally hidden from everyday sight. In a reading, this card may refer to the user, or to one whom they consult. It therefore suggests that you may yourself be gifted with the diviner's skill, so that when the cards are laid before you, you may be able to see at a glance the meaning shown there. If such is the case, be aware that this gift comes with a price—that you need to look even more carefully at what you see. More often than not, you will find that a second layer of meaning lies beneath the surface of your awareness, and that the ease with which you read the cards may be hiding a deeper story. Above all, you are likely to find that the interpretation you make points toward consequences and further outcomes, often far ahead of your initial search. If the card refers to another person, it suggests that an outside vision may be helpful in bringing you the answers you seek. The card is closely linked with the one that follows it, Truth, for this reason.

Reversed, you may find that your ability can be clouded by events, by the influence of others, or by a failure to grasp the true meaning of a reading. You may wish to discount the answers you get, preferring to go with your own vision. This is yet another aspect of divining that requires careful study and consideration. You may find that adjunct cards clarify this situation, lending clarity to what may otherwise be a darkened understanding.

Keywords Upright: Definition. Seeking meaning. Perceiving the source of things. Perceiving consequences. The outcome of things.

Keywords Reversed: Failure to see clearly. Dismissal of answers. Misunderstanding the potential of the search.

40: TRUTH

Truth is not always what it seems. We can be offered truths in a variety of contexts: religious, spiritual, news, traditional verities to which a group or individual may subscribe and offer it to others who will listen. False truths exist just as what we term "fake news" in our time, but which have been known by another word, propaganda, for far longer. It has been said that we must always weigh truth for ourselves, as a part of the freedom every living being has. The dictionary definition speaks of events that are in alignment with fact and physical evidence—but who is to say when a fact is true or not, or what physical evidence exists that cannot be manipulated to mean something else? Truth is shadowy and may appear solid when it is in fact insubstantial. In this card we see someone looking for the truth, perhaps seeing it set before them and yet remaining unsure if it is actual truth or an illusion. Often we see things in the mirror of life that seem to us to be true, but of which, when we take time to consider, we may be less certain. Shared values are important here for the way in which they influence our perception of what is true and what is not. In a reading, this card offers us "a" truth rather than "the" truth. It suggests we need to look below the surface appearance before clasping it to ourselves and building events around it. Be careful of who offers truth and what they mean by it. When real truth is encountered, you are likely to feel it in such a way that the idea of rejecting it seems impossible. But remember always to question what you feel and see, and check adjacent cards in your spread to see if the truth you seek is discoverable and acceptable.

Reversed, we may feel absolute certainty when presented with a truth that seems common to all. When someone tells you we are all alive, we may feel that this is an unquestionable truth. But when we ask ourselves what life is, we may wonder if the definitions are true or not. As in its upright position the card raises the question of what truth is, in its reversed position it suggests that all truths are true and that we should accept them as such if we can. This does not proscribe our ability to say no, to exercise our freedom of choice, but it does want us to take a more hard line in accepting what is presented as true. In this it connects with the earlier card of The Believer, where we are shown to walk a fine line between truth and lie, and with The Questioner, who seeks to find answers at every turn.

Keywords Upright: The appearance of truth. Received wisdom. Integrity. Verity. Shared values. Belief.

Keywords Reversed: Unshakable evidence. Unfailing belief. Absolute certainty. Determination. Accessing truth at first glance.

41: THE CLOWN

The Clown is in reality a kind of False Fool, someone who causes laughter by showing themselves to be clumsy, chaotic, or misdirected—more often than not, to make unkind fun of others. The face may be painted on in the form of a smile, but beneath this The Clown may be angry, sad, or vindictive. It is in the sequence to show how close The Fool is to this character, and how important it is not to act clownishly, especially when seeking to overturn the balance of others. In a reading, he may represent a false friend who offers support with one hand while undermining your own situation with the other. Clowns were an important part of ritual in certain ancient cultures throughout the world; they represented a reversal of the normal order and a reference to the chaos preceding creation. More than The Fool or The Magician, this character is a Trickster, one who can both teach through strange wisdom and also mislead by offering inconsequential or mirthless laughter. When the card comes up in a reading, you should be wary of your own actions, as well as those of others, being careful not to use mockery as a weapon, which may all too easily turn against you. The Clown also represents the strange parallels that occur between joy and sorrow, life and death, positive and negative. The lopsided frown, the open and closed eye, and The Fool's bladder and the skull recall the links with

Shakespeare's clowns, which threw his darkest tales into relief. Only The Clown can teach The Fool how to turn one into the other, to walk a balanced path along the narrow path without falling off (unless to do so causes hilarity!).

Reversed, the humour and wisdom of the clown—backward logic, wild wisdom, and mirthful observance, represent an escape from the chaotic aspects of the clown. The smile is genuine, the laughter kindly, and the wit pointed. If you are given to clownish behaviour, this will change your approach; if you are the subject of cruel jests, this shows how the cruelty may become warmth and the wit wisdom.

Keywords Upright: Risible. Fall guy. Scapegoat. Trickster. Mockery. False friend. The False Fool. Unkindness. Harmful lies.

Keywords Reversed: Serious humour. Relief of laughter. True wit and wisdom. Honesty.

42: THE MOON

The Moon may have begun with a depiction of one of the classical goddesses of the moon, Diana or Phoebe, as in the 15th-century Visconti-Sforza deck, but for most decks since then, it has tended to show two towers with the moon rising between them and often including two dogs howling at the lunar sphere. In almost every instance from the Renaissance onward, the card has included a crayfish or crab, representing the zodiacal sign of Cancer, ruled by the moon. Here we see the spirit of the moon itself, dancing between two mountain peaks, caught up in the glorious urgency and delight of the moon's influence. Taken collectively, these ideas can be seen as referring to the tidal changes that occur during the progress of the moon from new to full and round again, which can affect us all in one way or the other. It also recognises the magical beauty of the moon and its uncanny light.

The oldest meanings for the card tended toward the negative, having to do with lunar madness and inconsistency and ruling over the tidal energies of human life, from the menstrual cycle to the actions of the sea. As such, in readings it has more to do with shifting fortunes, the rise and fall and sweep of human affairs. In this way it represents synchronicity, the way that seemingly unconnected events come together and are shown to influence each other. The ability to see these things is all part of the lunar character—often indicating a psychic ability in the reader. Needless to say, such abilities should always be treated with caution, as they can give rise to the other major aspect of this card—uncertainty, delusion, and even deception. This does not, of course, mean that people in general with psychic gifts should be treated with suspicion, merely that the visions we receive by this means need to be filtered and balanced by thoughtful consideration.

Reversed, the card points to a more extreme denial of anything "lunar," strange, unforeseen, or unlikely, and as with all mystical experiences, it is essential to balance the magical with the mundane, the mysterious with the everyday. This prevents unbalanced attitudes or behaviour. It is all too easy to get caught up in a whirlwind of extraordinary events, forgetting that ordinary life goes hand in hand with the miraculous.

Keywords Upright: Tidal change. Twilight. A period of increase. Hidden influences. Esoteric forces. Unconscious urges. Dreams. Mutability. Emotion. Tidal. Night. In phase.

Keywords Reversed: Inability to change. Overwhelmed by emotional tides. Out of phase. Error. Lies. A period of decline. Delusion. Madness. Instability. Fluctuation. Irrational behavior. Deception.

43: THE SUN

The Sun's radiant light pierces everything, sending its rays into darkness, illuminating the darkest chambers of the soul and the most abstruse ideas of the thinker. It is one of the single most unvarying images in the Tarot and has changed very little over the centuries. It refers to the constancy of the sun's power and energy, which continues around the year, even during winter, when it continues to give light even though its warmth is obscured. In many traditional Tarots, either one or two children are portrayed as playing beneath the life-giving rays of the sun—here we see a rider on a horse flying above the sun, celebrating the brilliance and wonder of the star's light. This can be seen as a reference to Icarus, who in Greek myth flew too close to the sun in wings made for him by his father, Daedalus. It links this card with The Downfall card and suggests the overconfidence and self-worship that can emerge in the character of any individual. As we would expect from an image so radiant with light, the primary meaning of this card is happiness, contentment, and joy unbounded. It signifies health, wealth, and a joyous acceptance of good things, which rain down on the reader like the drops of radiant dew pictured on many of the versions of this card. It offers well-being and suggests that you, personally, bring light and pleasure to whomever you meet. If you are engaged in any work, you are likely to be the centre of the place, the warm hub to which all others gravitate. Your general optimism inspires those around you and enables you to lighten even the darkest moments. In difficult situations the sun's light is always available to you, enabling you to perceive the true state of affairs and act accordingly.

Reversed, the meaning turns certainty into uncertainty, triumph into vanity, marriage into divorce, and all the goodness that is present in the upright position is drained away. Unhappiness can follow, obscuring the clarity required to overcome doubt and uncertainty. Though the light of the sun is still present, you cannot see it for the clouds that hang over you. You are likely to be self-centered and believe too completely in your abilities to entrance others. You may find yourself the victim of loneliness and discontent.

Keywords Upright: Warmth. Enlightenment. Happiness. Contentment. Joy unbounded. Health. Triumph. Material fortune. Friendship. Marriage. Success.

Keywords Reversed: Unhappiness. Vanity. Pride. Misunderstanding. Broken marriage. Discontent. Loneliness. Burnt out.

44: THE STAR

The Star in our time tends more often than not to mean a person whose skills and abilities make them shine out from the crowd. But we also continue to look to the heavens and hope to read the meanings written there. Astronomy and astrology were of central importance in the time when Tarot first emerged, and this is reflected in the interpretation of this card, together with the previous two in the sequence, as we enter the place in which the heavenly bodies exert their pull upon events. Indeed, so strongly interconnected are The Moon, The Sun, and The Star that they cannot easily be separated and thus retain their traditional placing in the sequence of *The Fool's New Journey Tarot*. The history of The Star is interesting. Most decks today represent it as a woman with two jars pouring water into a stream, with between five or seven stars in the sky behind her. She is thus generally identified as Aquarius, the Water Carrier, but in earlier decks the iconography suggests an identification either with the Morning Star (Lucifer or Venus) or with the Star of Bethlehem. Others have identified it with Sirius, the Dog Star, and the figure of Isis. Here we have chosen to show a dancer in the spotlight, symbolically representing you in your desire for success and clearer insight. In each instance, the meaning remains more or less the same. It is a universal sign of hope, the recognition of the individual light as the material of stardom. It is both the light of the stars and the inner light we each carry within us. Its deeper, under-lying meaning retains a connection with both fortune and prophecy. It signifies the rising of hope and positive feelings on your personal horizon, as well as in more general terms. It is thus a very well-aspected card for times when you are thinking of beginning a new enterprise, moving to a new place, or simply starting over. It has all the vigor and determination that such decisions warrant, and it puts you center stage—lit-erally the star of your own life.

Reversed, the card suggests a lack of the necessary vision to make the right choice, and that we should avoid making any irreversible decisions at this time. We are, in effect, seers who have lost the ability to see clearly. We may be dogged by bad luck or feelings of pessimism. The light of The Star may wane and we may fade from the scene just at the time when we most need to be seen and heard. Be careful not to be too stubborn when you should give way to circumstances. Be wary of hope-lessness and feelings of instability.

Keywords Upright: Hope. Expectation. Harmony. Prophecy. Peace. Healing. Gifts of light. Inspiration. Good luck. Idealism. Destiny. Confidence. Star quality.

Keywords Reversed: Disappointment. Pessimism. Bad luck. Stubbornness. Hopelessness. Instability.

45: NATURE

Nature is everywhere around us. Even if we live in a concrete city world, we cannot help noticing the trees that grow there, the grasses and plants that spring up along roadsides, the animals that are part of our lives, the birds outside the widow, the spiders and mice, and of course the creatures that share our space as beloved pets. All these are part of nature. In the image for this card, we represented the living face of nature, often known as the Green Man, in the form of a leaf. The face is one of calmness and passivity, but it hides a depth of spiritual strength that carries all before it. The Green Man is one of the oldest known symbols that exist. We find representations of it inscribed on the walls of caves from the earliest times of human existence, and we see it carved on rocks, cut into the earth, and, in more recent times, captured in stone in the great cathedrals of Europe. The presence of these figures, often hidden until recent times in the roofs of the stone buildings until modern lighting showed them, is evidence of a long-standing belief that the natural world has a face, and a voice, and that it speaks to us in leaf and flower, woodland and hillside, river and sea. It is there whether we like it or not, no matter how often we enter it fully. Here we show The Fool clinging to the stalk of the leaf, caught up in the energy of the natural world, which carries him on in his Journey. This is the essential meaning of this card. It refers to our relationship with

Nature, our ability to ignore it (often at our peril!), and its determination to continue reaching out to us wherever we are. Nature was here before humanity and will remain long after us—if we do not destroy it, and ourselves with it. We too, are part of Nature, natural beings who exist within the world only because nature exists. In recent times we have begun to learn the truth about the way we relate to the natural world—our determination to cut down forests, drain lakes and rivers, burrow ever deeper beneath the surface of the land, stamp our presence more and more on the natural world—often to its— and our—detriment, have become world news. In a reading, this card represents our relationship to Nature and to natural events—showing us that we perhaps need to give more attention to where and how we live. It is about the way we respond to our environment and whether we choose to care for it or ignore it. These things reach across every aspect of life and show us how we can best relate to the world in which we live, encouraging us to understand what an important part Nature has to play in everything we do.

Reversed, this is about an uncaring approach to Nature and natural events. Places marked as beauty spots, or places of rest and refreshment in nature, have no part in our lives, and we may exchange a sense of acceptance for a feeling of ownership. Whether tending a garden, caring for a plant in your home, or recognising your own place in the natural scheme of things, you may feel that this has no relevance to you. Be careful not to cling to this viewpoint too utterly—every one of us has a part to play in the survival of the natural world, and to dismiss it is to lose a huge part of our purpose in this life. Be aware too that an unnatural approach may lead to the failure of plans and dreams both for ourselves and others, and that we may be seeing only a part of a far-greater whole.

Keywords Upright: Natural. Whole. Environment. Refreshment. The circle of life. Caring for the world. Seeking the wisdom of Nature. Allowing ourselves to become part of the natural world.

Keywords Reversed: Unnatural. Divided. Separated. Banished. Seeing only part of the world. A sense of ownership of the natural world. Losing our connection to the whole circle of being.

46: THE LOST

The Lost. Who has not felt themselves to be one of these? We set out on our journeys full of hope and expectation, only to find that at some point we strayed from the path we were on and found ourselves somewhere we had not intended to be. Dante's great poem *The Divine Comedy* begins with the famous lines that say that "midway through this life I awoke to find myself in a great wood." There are so many ways to be lost amid the trees, so many turnings and branches from The Road (card 52), so many doors to open, some labelled, others not. Life is full of surprises, choices, decisions, any one of which may take us into a place that we neither know nor understand (see card 1: The Maze). Not only can we lose our way on the road, so too can we be lost to ourselves in our thoughts and understanding. Life can seem more opaque, less easy to read, the older we get. Age does not necessarily bring wisdom, and even the most devoted explorer can admit to being lost. Thus we made this card to express the feelings or situations in which we find ourselves shaking our heads and murmuring: I'm lost. In a reading it expresses the way we feel at such times, blindly turning to each direction, looking into futures we cannot know, exploring the various possibilities we think may bring us back into focus. If you are feeling rudder-less, lost at sea, washed up on a strange shore, look to the cards next to this one. Where do they suggest you go to find yourself?

What must you do to unscramble the messages from the universe that seem to contradict your every thought and action?

Reversed, you may feel that you have found yourself at last, perhaps after a long search. The path suddenly looks more brightly lit; the doors seem ready to open and are clearly labelled. Friends or allies wave to and beckon you onward. From being a card of lost ways and opportunities, it is suddenly a card of discovery, awakening, confidence. Who has not wished for a clear map to guide them through life? Such things may well exist and be awaiting discovery. With this you are lost no more.

Keywords Upright: Opportunities not taken. Decisions. Without a guide or map. Unprepared. Rudderless. Lost. Forgetful of your goals.

Keywords Reversed: Discovery. More options. Clarity. Strength of purpose. Knowing who you are and what you seek. A clear map.

47: JUDGEMENT

Judgement, also known as Last Judgement and The Angel, is a formidable archetype in the sequence of classical Major Arcana. Most traditional decks, from the earliest time to the present, depict this as an angel blowing a trumpet to awaken the sleeping dead to rise and follow him to heaven. In some, God also appears, flanked by two angels, again calling home the faithful. In the context of the Tarot this image is a uniquely Christian one, as this is the only religion that suggested that the dead would arise in their physical bodies. Prior to this, only the beliefs of ancient Egypt suggested the need for a physical vessel to contain the spirit—hence the tradition of mummification. Later imagery is far starker and often included grizzly images of skeletons or partially rotting bodies emerging from the ground. For most readers today, it is more likely to be seen as a call to rise, not to heaven but to a new direction or purpose in life. Rather, as in the card of Death, it does not refer to a physical state but to an inner one. The question of judgement will be seen differently by each individual, and thus we have depicted the Egyptian goddess Isis, who measured the weight of souls against a feather, learning in this way whether the individual had acted well or negatively in their life or if they were weighed down by the presence of cruel or uncaring actions. Some have seen this as referring to a judgemental figure or organization that has power over them; others may see it as their own inner judge, setting out the pros and cons of the situation and requiring them to decide for themselves on the appropriate action. In most readings, depending on adjacent cards, Judgement reflects a need for change—just how radical will depend on the nature of the issue and the circumstances surrounding it. It can be a plain and simple change of approach to the way you view a situation, or a far more earth-shattering call to change the direction of your life. The card often appears at a time when you may be at a crossroads and need to make the appropriate decision as to which path to take, on the basis of your own judgement.

Reversed, the card indicates a difficulty in reaching a clearly defined decision and an inability to change or acknowledge the need for change. It also suggests that you may be overly self-critical, which can prevent movement of any kind. You may seek to postpone actions until a better time comes along, but this can result in your becoming stuck, waiting for something that may never happen. Self-judgement can be both harsh and isolating; you may see yourself in such a negative light that you become burdened with thoughts that may not be a true reflection of your personality or process.

Keywords Upright: Change. Judgement. Self-assessment. Strong opinions. Outcome. Promotion. Decision. Restoration. Weighing the possibilities. Beginning again. Return.

Keywords Reversed: Stasis. Postponement. Weakness. Disappointment. Procrastination. Alienation. Delay. Indecision.

48: THE LISTENERS

The Listeners are those people who are able not just to listen but also to hear. This may seem a strange distinction, but it is all too easy to listen to what you are being told but not to hear or understand it. In the image you will see the sound wave that each one of The Listeners is attending to. Each will hear something different. Just as no single card image will be perceived in the same way by everyone, so it is with hearing. Did someone say "natural" or "unnatural"? What did you hear and what effect did this have on your understanding? This is something that all users and readers of Tarot need to be aware of. If you receive an answer that fills you with foreboding, do you take it on board or convince yourself it can't be right and that you should therefore ignore it? Equally, if reading for a client, you may see an answer that is very negative, and you may need to consider how you deal with this. As with all divinatory devices, asking a question invites an answer, and these are not always what we would like to hear. However, the best advice is that which we truly listen to and understand.

Reversed, this indicates someone who does not listen—not only in the sense of not hearing the words and their meaning, but also of not wanting to be given advice that they would rather not hear. As noted above, this is often a difficult decision to make—but if you truly want to know the answer to your enquiry, you need to listen and respond accordingly. There is also a sense of losing attention here, or drifting off into a place where you cannot hear what is being said. Those who love music but do not in actuality hear it are also an indication of an inability to hear what is being implied by the sounds you hear.

Keywords Upright: Paying attention. Deeply focused. Witnessing. Hearing what is true. Contemplation. Music.

Keywords Reversed: Ignoring what you hear. Loss of attention. Hearing only what you wish to hear. Lack of focus. Inability to hear tunes.

49: HISTORY

History is a series of echoes that resound through time. It can teach us so much that we neglect at our peril. How many times have events followed the same patterns—especially when these lead to war and suffering? We are far more likely to ignore the past and the lessons it can teach, preferring to think that our realisations of the moment are more important; yet, to spend time in the presence of History is to discover clues that can help us today. This is not just on the great scale of world events, but also in our personal lives. Have we made mistakes that could be rectified with hindsight? Are there patterns to observe in our daily lives that point toward mistakes we have made and should not make again? We are often advised to live in the present, and this certainly helps us avoid dwelling on past events or looking into the future for things we hope will work out. But we can learn to see the shape of history without needing to dwell upon it; it can and does outline ways to prevent repetition. This relates to our ancestral bequest—the echoes of events that are part of our family history, and from which we may learn. The ancient world understood the importance of history; the Greeks, Mesopotamians, Arkadians, and Egyptians all possessed gods who oversaw historic events: Inanna in Mesopotamia, Naram-Sin in Akkad, Horus and Aten in Egypt, and Athena and Apollo in Greece all saw the shapes and pattens of human history and sometimes intervened to being about a different conclusion (see card 2: The Believer).

This tended toward prophecy rather than history, but within the myths of these ancient deities the golden thread of history is ever present. In most early mythic visions, at least one aspect of the gods and goddesses who are part of the pattern of history are weavers. History itself is the weaver of time and events, bringing together people or situations that might otherwise never have met. It literally shapes our lives and should always be recognised as having a part to play in the way we live now. Thus, in a reading it will point the way toward a deeper assessment of the situation, perhaps with a backward look at our own personal histories.

Reversed, the card refers, even more than in its upright position, to our failure to recognise the lessons of history, our dismissal of its relevance to us as individuals, and a turning away from the life lessons delivered by our personal histories. This suggests that we need to look more carefully at the history of actions we are about to take. Did we act in this way before, and what was the result? We should also look for shapes that stand out in the larger pattern of events. How do the actions we are considering affect others? These are all part of history's ability to create pattens in the chaos of life (see card 27: Chaos).

Keywords Upright: Comparison. Reverberation. Resonance. Replaying. Echoes. Ripples. Repetition. Old ways that seem dead. A source of our identity.

Keywords Reversed: Ignoring the lessons of the past. Turning away from our own history. Shapes and patterns. Cause and effect.

50: THE OBSERVER

The Observer is that part of our consciousness that keeps watch over our actions. It looks at patterns of behaviour, attitudes toward love, work, the environment, relationships—at every aspect of life as we live it. It does not judge, and it is not our conscience, but it does bring to the fore ideas that may otherwise be lost amid the whirlwind of activity, and purpose that drives us to follow our instinct. In some ways, The Observer *is* our instinct, given form and authority so that when it appears, we are more likely to listen. In a reading, it suggests that we take care to observe everything that is a part of our goal—not just the clear and obvious things, but the smaller aspects that are so often overlooked or considered unimportant. The Observer lives at the deepest level of our consciousness, tapping into the root causes of behaviour and the reasoning part of our brain that affects the way we behave and our attitude to whatever issue dominates the current moment. It helps us see the whole picture, gives us access to the critiquing self that assesses our responses to being, and (sometimes) shows us a way to respond that resolves matters with less anxiety. It helps us assess the issue clearly and suggests that we consider the cards that are adjacent in the spread with clearer thought and greater concern.

Reversed, it refers more to the signs we fail to notice or take action for or against. It is blindly proceeding without care and attention, letting our deepest longing govern our process to the extent that we tend to do nothing. The Observer within gives us signs to follow, nudges us into action, but when it is ignored, it fails and dwindles until we are driven to act according to our baser instincts. It can also be a source of anxiety, prompting us to go over the same ground many times without settling on a viable answer.

Keywords Upright: Vigilance. Observing. Seeing the whole picture. Critique. Assessing. Watching. Concern for detail. Overseer.

Keywords Reversed: Failure to see patterns. Doing nothing. Circumventing inner promptings. Following our baser instincts.

51: THE OCEAN

The Ocean holds so much that is essential to our lives. It is a container of vast and often-unfathomable secrets, truths and patterns that affect us every day. As we came from the waters millennia ago, so we still feel the pull of the tides when the moon is full, causing our own inner tidal selves to react (see card 42: The Moon). The presence of a huge number of deities who watch over or live in the oceans of the world makes it clear how the importance of the seas was recognised from the earliest times. These are the manifestations of the primal waters from which we emerged, and are still seen as having a powerful effect upon us. To sail on the oceans' back, whether in a vast ocean liner or a simpler sailboat, puts us in touch with the infinite depths of creation. We may think of Roman Neptune with his chariot pulled by seahorses, or, in the Greek pantheon, of Doris, the goddess of the sea's bounty, or Leukothea, whom sailors invoked for protection in times of distress, or, in Slavic mythology, Morskoy Tsar, the god king of the sea. All are deities who are the source of vast richness of wisdom and strength. Nor must we forget the creatures who dwell in our seas, from the fish that feed us as they have from the beginning of humanity, to the vast intelligences of whales, dolphins, and manta rays, whose presence is a constant reminder of the wealth of The Ocean. Just as the seas themselves are among the most powerful forces in our world, so those who represent them offer resources that can bring much to a reading. When this card is drawn, it raises the level of energy and support of any of those around it. It can also mean a journey of great distance across the sea, or a literal "sea change" in our lives. Here then is a vast resource of wisdom and strength that can aid us in our every task. There is still a primordial reaction to the danger of the deep.

Reversed, The Ocean becomes a bottomless place where sharks and monsters lurk, manifesting in our lives as unforeseen dangers, unexpected reversals, or the loss of our sense of belonging to the source of life and energy. The seas still contain many things of which we have little or no awareness, and in readings these may emerge as blocking our way, threatening the shape of our lives or the outcome of whatever endeavour we may be engaged upon. It is still the source of life but may turn against us.

Keywords Upright: Immensity. The unfathomable. The source of life. Depth of vision. Distance overseas. Feeding us with wonder.

Keywords Reversed: Negative forces at work. Lurking monsters. Breaking links with the source of life. Blocking our way.

52: THE ROAD

The Road leads us onward toward our goals. It can lead us into new paths, new understandings, fresh observation, and realisation. It can also lead us where we neither expect nor desire to go, sometimes at a cost to our endeavours. But above all, it centres on our sense of direction, the inner compass that guides our steps whether we realise it or not. Roads connect things, points on a map, beginnings and ends of a journey, understandings that may change as we walk it. The Road is also our path of discovery, the personal way that we take, from our first steps to the endings of our journey, and here we see The Fool himself making his way along it. He seems a little uncertain, perhaps, having come so far. What lies ahead? Yet, we see that he is ready for whatever may come. The Road is also an indicator of where we are on our path; we may lose our way and end up somewhere we did not intend to be, but this is why we need to observe the way as far as possible, both behind and ahead. The card suggests turnings and changes, just as it can also point to reaching a long-sought goal. Inevitably, roads are connected and guarded by a variety of deities who were called upon to protect and advise travellers on the way. In Roman mythology we find Abeona, the goddess of outward journeys, who protects travellers and also watches over the steps of young children in particular, seeing to it that they do not stumble. Her sister is Adiona, the goddess of safe return. Together, they watch over the road and journeys we take. Many also called upon Apollo, who drove the chariot of the sun and was therefore considered important to ensure a safe journey. Remembering how important roads are is a useful strategy, and in a reading it may point to the need to change direction, even to aim for a different goal. We may indeed miss our turning and find ourselves stuck in a cul-de-sac.

Reversed, The Road may lead us astray, taking us to places that offer no positive outcome. We can lose our way so easily if we forget that our steps are guarded and guided by the deities of The Road. Here they may lead you down roads that go nowhere, or even to places where you risk losing your way for good. This can also refer to negative reactions of a more general kind, when our steps falter and we make the wrong decisions just as we may take the wrong turnings. This leads to us literally losing our purpose, or direction that leads us toward whatever goal we are seeking.

Keywords Upright: The way. The path beneath your feet. The status quo. Direction. Honour. Learning the truth. Homecoming journeys. Carefree travellers. The open road. Casting off burdens.

Keywords Reversed: The wrong way. Missed turnings. Negative reactions. Blind turnings. Loss of direction.

53: WISDOM

Wisdom is the cousin of Truth (card 40) and the sister of Knowledge. It offers a way of discovery that may be latent in us but requires encouragement to manifest. It offers the gifts of understanding, of ethical behaviour, and it allows us to live lives in tune with the universe. It is also full of contrariness, often ungraspable in its complexity yet perceivable in a moment in its simplicity. In certain Eastern religions the concept of "crazy wisdom" suggests that the master who embodies the teachings may have reached a point where wisdom itself appears strange and where the teachings seem contrary. This seems to sit well with The Fool, whose own wisdom can be said to be crazy, and suggests a degree of humility that may seem unwise but is in fact full of wisdom. Knowledge is part of Wisdom but not always as closely connected as we may think. Knowledge can be deceitful and lead us to unwise behaviour or decisions, while Wisdom steers us to a better understanding and more appropriate actions, because Wisdom lies at the heart of knowledge as the matrix of all creation. This is why, in so many cultures, there is always a god or goddess of wisdom, whether it be Athena, the civilising goddess of wisdom in Greek tradition; or, in Mesopotamia, Innana, who descends to the otherworld in order to gain wisdom; or Prometheus (forethought), who comes to rescue humankind from being without its own gift and brings fire to help us learn the necessary technology to live. In his case, as with many of the wisdom divinities, there is a sacrifice to be made for mediating divine knowledge to humanity. Prometheus is chained to a rock and has an eagle pecking at his liver, while Innana descends to the otherworld, stripping herself of her own garments and adornments, to be hung on a hook. Wisdom always comes with a cost, yet Isis, whose husband is cut into many pieces, gathers them together so that she might conceive a child. This becomes a metaphor for gathering lost knowledge and reembodying it for the benefit of everyone. To be godlike in wisdom is also to have suffered and to be willing to be of service. Wisdom never acts for its own self—it is a common factor of all people, institutions, and cultures to have this necessary custodial ability to mediate for the benefit of all, without regard to sex, age, or station. Wisdom is indeed the first democracy. But we have lived through many eras where wisdom was taken into private and privileged possession, and where everyone else was excluded and kept in ignorance. Many myths speak of wisdom's cloak being rent into pieces because an exclusive cast determines to own wisdom—which is inalienably free. Who serves wisdom serves the universe. A true philosopher—literally a lover of wisdom—knows that wisdom cannot belong to them, because it serves us all. In a reading this card may sum up everything we know or feel that we know, pointing us toward the gifts of forethought and knowledge offered by the cards surrounding it.

Reversed, we may see what appears to be a lack of wisdom, foolish and thoughtless behaviour, or even the giving away of one's own natural wisdom in the face of contrary advice or belief. Perhaps your issue is with perceived wisdom, which seems contrary to your personal approach? Are you a seeker of wisdom or one who finds it difficult to accept the knowledge of others? As with the upright readings, there is much that seems unclear or uncertain. Wisdom is not won easily.

Keywords Upright: The sum of knowledge. Practical life lived in tune. The ethical path we follow. Understanding. The theft of knowledge. Danger of too-little wisdom. Suffering to obtain wisdom. Creation.

Keywords Reversed: Lack of wisdom. Blindness to good advice. Giving away your wisdom. Trying to own wisdom.

54: FEAR

Fear brings us to a halt. It freezes our every movement and thought. It takes up residence in our minds and switches our every movement to flight mode. It stops us in our tracks and shuts all the doors and windows, locks all doors, and throws away the key. If we allow it to, it will rule our lives and stop our progress, making every task seem overwhelming and impossible. Small hills become mountains, a walk to the end of the street feels like a 5-mile hike, and the very idea of making a decision fills us with such terror that we are lost. When it appears in a reading, it stands for everything we fear about the outcome of the issue. Whatever positive thoughts you had are suddenly reversed, with only a difficult and painful outcome possible. You may feel indecisive, shaky, diffident, and uncertain what action to take. Be aware of the cards before and after this card in the reading, as these will mitigate the effects of the fear and offer ways to progress despite it. In classical Greek mythology, fear is named Phobos (from which we derive the word *phobia*). He is the son of Ares (god of war) and Aphrodite (goddess of love), his brother is Deimos (terror), and his sister is Eric (discord). We can see from this how fear exerts its hold. It induces fear of war (not just armed conflict but wars of attrition between friends, relatives, or companies), builds terror into our viewpoint, and sows discord on every side until we no longer feel we can turn anywhere for support. It is interesting to note that the gods are all children of Love and War, where we can easily find cause for fear.

Reversed, the picture changes. Fear is banished or at least reduced to a manageable degree. Stasis is broken and you can think again. Instead of being fearful, you may explore a degree of caution, advising you against taking risks, but forward motion is restored along with self-confidence and hope (card 34: Hope, which in this deck balances Fear). Those who seemed to be attacking you are now helpers and supporters. Looking ahead, you see ways of escaping the trap in which fear had locked you.

Keywords Upright: Stasis. Frozen. Fearful. Inability to move. Indecision. Avoidance of issues. Imobility.

Keywords Reversed: Relief. Light at the end of the tunnel. Belief in the self, restored. Movement permitted. Hope granted.

55: THE PAST

The Past may hold secrets we have sought always, yet we tend to dismiss it as something without power or meaning for us now. Looking back is useless, we are told; look to the future for your answers. But the past is a mighty book, one that holds many keys to life. Delving into it, we find an endless pattern of events that mirror our own. These may be world-shattering things such as war, pestilence, or any number of fearful events. But alongside these are the problems faced by others throughout time, the seemingly small issues that we find huge and overwhelming. Imagine if you could find someone in the past who understood exactly what you needed to know. Perhaps you can. Somewhere inside of us exists ancestral memory, fragments of lives long since turned to dust that have left their markers in our blood. This card reminds us of that fact and urges us to let our thoughts go deeper than previously, until they reach a place where memory awakens in us and we begin to recall the past. In a reading, this card reminds us of possibilities from our own past, or those of others who perhaps faced the same problem. The cards surrounding this may point in which direction you should be looking. Remember to look at the causes and effects of past choices. See what you might do better, and celebrate where you are now in the lineage of your family and the decisions you made to bring you to this point.

Reversed, we see the past as a place of memories we seek to forget. The lessons we once learned are seen as without value. Our past is dead to us, and we seek only the future and the better times it promises to hold. Where we had looked to the ancestral wisdom of earlier times, now we turn away from these in search of new things we see as more positive. In a reading, this says to us: Look over the hill at the land beyond; forget the old roads you walked. Here the figure of the present is walking away from the past. It suggests you should look for fresh pastures and learn the new lessons that life offers. This can be a positive thing, of course, but it has its own dark side. Cutting yourself off from your past can be as destructive as turning your back on life itself, and especially on those who offer memories of other times.

Keywords Upright: Remembering past times. Considering options. How could we do better? Celebrating the outcome of past efforts. Analysing cause and effect.

Keywords Reversed: Forgetting the lessons of the past. Seeking new ventures without consideration. Letting go of things that mattered. Looking for new favourites.

56: THE FUTURE

The Future fascinates us. We study it and contemplate it all the time—often without even realising it. The Past we can see if we look carefully enough, but The Future? What does that hold for us? Many diviners will expect a Tarot or other type of oracle to answer this question: What does the future hold for me? Only rarely do we get clear answers to such questions. The Future is being written as we think of it. At the moment it does not exist; what exists is now. We can make guesses, and divinatory devices such as this one can give us clues, but in reality it is better to ask about what the future "might" look like for us, rather than expecting a picture of ourselves five, ten, or even fifty years from now. This also brings up the issue of what we choose to believe. Suppose you do a reading about the future and receive a warning not to travel. Do you take the advice or ignore it? This is one of the reasons why most diviners will always advise you not to ask direct questions. The Tarot is simply a deck of cards, not a magic wand, and it can and does offer guidance—but most of this is to confirm things you already instinctively know. The future is opaque and hard to grasp, but we can ask for guidelines to help us prepare for what may become—and let's note the "may," because nothing is certain and two readings taken on successive days will usually be different. This is because the future is not mapped out for us. We make choices every day that alter the balance of our lives. The Fool must learn this on his journey and does so by letting his mind drift into new patterns and realisations while continuing to journey into the future. He learns to be aware of sudden and unexpected twists or blockages in the road, as we too should try to do. He sees the star of the future shining through the uncertain clouds. The best advice of this card could be expressed as this: Look where you are going. Don't trip over unseen obstacles but don't be constantly looking for them as you go. The balance required to do this is not as hard as you may think.

Reversed, the card suggests we may be too sure of the future—that we are looking for something that matches a pattern only we can see. Our futures become stagnant and stuck as they refuse to follow the road ahead that we have laid out for ourselves. This can also mean that we are unprepared for unexpected events and thus even less able to deal with the future as it occurs.

Keywords Upright: Looking ahead. Considering options. Hoping for the future. Looking beyond the present. Uncertainty. Feeling lost.

Keywords Reversed: Confusion. Misreading certainty. Unwariness. Being too decisive.

57: HEALING

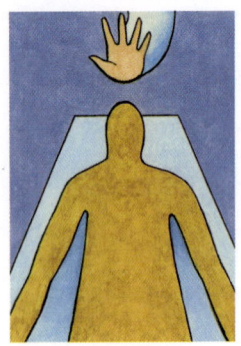

Healing is something we all need at some period in our lives. It may be physical or spiritual, and we may look in many different places to find it. Essentially we are looking for ways to be whole, to salvage the parts of our lives that the more brutal aspects of being may have taken from us or made us see in a negative light. Receiving healing is not as easy as it may seem. If we are sick, we hope for something to make us better, whether we see a medical or alternative practitioner. To take the medication offered may bring about the desired effect, but at times our bodies choose to reject what we have been given. Above all, we should be willing and open to receive the healing proffered. If we are not able to do this, then the healing may not work. At such times we need to look inward at the causes of our illness. We often forget the miraculous quality of the body to repair itself. Easy enough to see if we break a bone, but less easy when a clear reason for feelings of sickness or sorrow attack us without discoverable cause. We need to look beyond the surface at such times, and in a reading this is more often the message of the card. Whatever you seek, whether it is a happy and fulfilling relationship, a good job, or the satisfactory outcome to a long-cherished plan, these things can reflect a need for healing that goes beyond flesh and bone.

Reversed, the healing offered may not be what we need, and can actually make us worse. Sometimes the mind itself gets in the way. This does not mean that we should reject the help of a healer outright, only that we should consider the long-term effects of the healing on our lives. The card suggests we may be feeling fragmented and listless, even that we are losing hope of finding the solution we need, or that we are estranged from life as we have lived it to date. Remember that this effects not only our physical well-being but can turn a deeply held desire sour and prevent us from receiving healing in the way we should.

Keywords Upright: Searching for health. Becoming whole. Restoring mind, body, and spirit. Energised. Actively seeking healing. Responding to healthful living.

Keywords Reversed: Rejecting healing. Feeling fragmented and listless. Losing hope. Estrangement from life. Failure to receive healing.

58: THE WORLD

The World is generally accepted as referring to completion—to the final glorious moments of the world before it becomes transcendent. Tarot expert Paul Huson suggested that it may at one time have come before Judgement and represented the last in a cosmic sequence of Sun, Moon, Star, and Earth, with the final card representing the calling forth of the whole world to transcend existence. It is the moment at the end of the Grail Quest, when the successful seekers are permitted to either look into the vessel or drink from it, after which it is returned to its temple to await the next seekers. As in this myth, the underlying meaning of the card is that we have come full circle in our search for answers. In *The Fool's New Journey Tarot*, there is only one further step to take—from completion of the journey into the realm of Eternity. The card is thus mostly about the triumph—over adversity, trials, tests, and problems. It is the card of success, of coming home, of completion. Whether your journey has been one of life-changing complexity or a simple request concerning an everyday issue, this card tells you that you have completed that part of the journey and that the outcome is a good one. More than that, it implies that you yourself are a complete person, that you have balanced the conflicts that surround us everywhere and brought your journey to a harmonious conclusion, a place from which you may review everything that has ever happened to you, and catch a glimpse of the road before you. For such a person the way is clear—others will follow you when they perceive your success. Your health is good, your perception sharpened to a point of intensity. You are the center around which everything else revolves.

Reversed, the opposite of the above is true. Stagnation, inertia, and a general loss of vision attend. Plans made come to nothing; we become mired in a bog of our own creation and cannot find a way out. Neglected obligations, failure to complete tasks you have set for yourself or that others have set for you, bring your journey to an end. There is literally nowhere else to go without help.

Keywords Upright: The world. Completion. Reward. Universal truth. Time. The seasons. Attainment. Success. Great change. Liberation. Flowering. The context of life. The full blueprint. Living life to the full.

Keywords Reversed: Inertia. Stagnation. Loss of vision. Failure. Delayed completion. Prolongation. Time running out.

59: ETERNITY

Eternity is a big word that describes a vast possibility—that a larger plan exists than we are aware of, and that by stepping beyond the limitations of time and space we may come to terms with all eventualities and discoveries to come. The normal sequence in Tarot ends with The World—sometimes The Completed World—implying that this is the summation of all things, the coming together of plans and their successful implementation. The Eternity card takes this idea a step further—largely into unknown regions, although we may still look into a future without form and catch glimpses of what may be. It tells us that there may be more to life than we have so far experienced and that possibilities are literally endless. It is a card that includes everything, all that has passed and will be, all our dreams and hopes, which continue to exist even when we think there is no viable response or action we can take. The lemniscate that encircles the head of the person in this image is a symbol of eternity dating back to classical Greece and the work of the philosopher Proclus. It shows that all time is connected and that everything extends from everything in a constant ribbon of activity and life. In a reading, it tells us we need to look beyond immediate circumstances and accept that there is more to life than may appear to us. It offers a wider perspective on every issue we raise, irrespective of the adjacent cards. It tells us to widen our horizons, to look beyond the obvious, and to allow our dreams to fully manifest.

Reversed, our vision narrows, limiting all options and suggesting we may have lost the direction we sought. What seems open and momentous now seems small and circumscribed. These thoughts derive from our own sense if insecurity, which we must seek to turn aside if we are to grow and achieve the limitless potential offered by the card in an upright opposition. As ever with these expansive cards, we need to look carefully at the adjacent images and perceive how they may relate, strengthening or weakening the absolute impressions of Eternity.

Keywords Upright: Timelessness. Looking ahead. Wider perspectives. Unbound possibilities. Inclusion of all. Passing beyond. Accepting there is more to life. Absolutes.

Keywords Reversed: Timebound. Narrowing vision. Limited opportunities. Exclusion of wonder. Loss of direction. Sense of limitation. Diminished options.

CARD BACK

The Full Circle

Here we see The Fool, caught in the midst of his journey, dancing around the world while surrounded by the circling clouds that were within him at the beginning. This brings the story full circle and shows how it leads through all the elements of the 60 cards of *The Fool's New Journey Tarot*. Again, as with classic Tarot, the card back is designed to be read upright or reversed, with no clue to either until the card is flipped over.

PART
TWO

THE FOOL'S STORY

Fool Waking

Fool woke in the morning
met a bird on the way
bade the bird good day
Fool
with a kick
made air his own

Fool
woke in the evening
sang a song
slept
his song kept going
till morning was again

THE FOOL'S JOURNEYS—
OLD AND NEW—TOLD AS FABLES

Beginning at the Beginning

As with any new Tarot deck, the best way to begin is to familiarise yourself with the meanings. Even if you are a regular reader, you can still learn new interpretations. In this deck, you have a little more to learn, as there are new cards not included in the traditional decks, and in addition, some of the meanings of the classical cards have shifted to make it at one with the new trumps. You will also find new things in the iconography of the cards, including the traditional ones. For instance, in the Death card there is a different kind of image from that more usually linked with its interpretation. So to begin at the beginning, you literally need to work your way through each card, including the classic ones, and learn not only what they mean but what they show.

To help with this process, I have written two stories, or fables, which follow here. These are designed to illustrate the differences between the traditional Tarot sequence and this wholly new sequence of *The Fool's New Journey Tarot*. They both were written intuitively, by simply looking at the images and following the ideas that arose from them. Some, therefore, reflect traditional meanings attributed to classic Tarot, while others will seem completely different—and those observant readers may see occasional parallels between this new sequence and the traditional one.

I found that working on these taught me a great deal more about the sequence—indeed, about Tarot itself—that I had spent so long toiling over, and the meanings of certain individual cards. Two or three of these changed places as I went, falling into what seems now to be a natural progression from 0 to 60. Of course, anyone may do a reading of this kind and will find their own meanings and stories within them. Indeed, I encourage all the users of this Tarot to do that very thing. It's the best way to learn the meanings of the new cards, and it can teach you a great deal more. I plan to produce a book explaining this in greater detail, which will follow soon. Meantime, sit back, open your deck, and read, looking at each card as you go and seeing the parallels, differences, twists, and turns provided by the cards themselves. Compare the variations between the traditional and the new and see where these lead you. In short, let the stories here lead you in a journey of your own, deeper into the world of *The Fool's New Journey Tarot*.

THE FOOL'S OLD JOURNEY

(A Fable Told by Tarot)

(i)

Here's the Dreamer's Apprentice, learning to follow the magic of his innermost being on a road to somewhere/nowhere.

On this night he dreams of a rainbow, a bridge from dream to dream, and a dog. The dog is small and noisy. It wakes him from his dream, he thinks. He finds he's been sleeping on a cliffside, a drop that falls away to nothing. Then he understands: he doesn't understand anything. He doesn't know who or what he is. What's in a name? What's in a game? He looks at the dog and the dog looks back. Its tongue lolls out. It barks again and tugs at his trouser leg. He looks at the rainbow and sees it's a bridge. The dog runs a few steps ahead. It wants him to follow. So he does, stepping into the bridge and finding his footing truly. He looks ahead and sees another cliff across the nothingness. It seems to have a road that leads somewhere. Whereto? He has no idea. The dog barks and leads the way. He follows. He's awake, he thinks, but it all feels like a dream. But what's a dream anyway? He doesn't know. He follows the dog.

(ii)

He's across the bridge. There's not much light, just enough to see the path ahead, some trees, and vague shadows. The dog is eager. It runs ahead, returns to him, runs ahead again. Slowly it grows lighter. The path gets wider. Now in front of him is a village: a street of shambling houses, a rutted road. He finds himself standing in the square. There's no one about. The dog runs in circles for a while, then starts barking at a man he sees, sitting behind a table off to one side. He's laying out cards in rows on the tabletop, picking them up, turning them over, laying them down again. His hands move as quick as light. The Fool—if Fool he is—goes over to take a look. The man never stops moving the cards around. They're strange cards, with pictures on them. They look familiar, but The Fool can't remember where he's seen them before.

The man behind the table is called The Magician. He's a trickster, stealing bits of people's souls, hiding the truth from them. He looks at The Fool; The Fool looks at him. The man starts laying out some more cards. The Fool sees himself on them. Moving, walking along a road. There's a dog at his heels.

He stares down at the cards, wondering. They look so shiny and nice. It seems this is a game he could play. He reaches out toward the cards. At that moment a woman appears at his side. "Don't do that," she says, "or you'll lose your soul." The man behind the desk stops moving the cards for a moment. The woman reaches out and takes The Fool's hand. Everything goes fuzzy. When his eyes clear, he's standing inside a big stone building, with long, narrow windows filled with coloured glass. Sunlight falls through them and makes patterns on the floor. The Fool goes and stands in the patterns. They transfer themselves to him. Now he's a Fool in a motley suit of many colours. It pleases him a lot.

The lady comes toward him. She is dressed in purple and wears white gloves. Her eyes shine like stars. She looks at him. "That was very Foolish of you," she says. "You could have lost your soul. You need some lessons about life. Follow me."

The Fool looks at her. Suddenly the dog is there, jumping around and barking loudly. The lady looks down at the dog and smiles. "I am an enchantress," she says, "though some call me Priestess. Your dog is very protective." "Don't worry," she says to the dog. "Everything is fine." She starts walking away and The Fool follows, with the dog at his heels. It stops barking.

As they go, the big stone building seems to get bigger, as if it was stretching away into the distance. Somewhere away over there are two thrones—big stone thrones. On them sit two splendid people. The Fool looks at them in wonder. He's never seen anything quite so marvellous. The Enchantress stops and turns to him. "Let me introduce you," she says. "This is The Emperor of Time, and this is The Empress of Love. They take care of all the worlds, and they are certainly very wise."

The Fool looks at the two wonderful people. He thinks he ought to ask them some questions, but he can't think of any. He feels rather Foolish. The Emperor looks down at him: "Do you understand about time?" he asks. The Fool shakes his head. He can't remember what time it is.

"Time is everywhere and nowhere," says The Emperor. "Everyone is always rushing about because they think they never have enough time. If only they realised that the more time they take, the more time they have. Do you understand about time?" Somehow The Fool finds himself nodding. He's not quite sure if he does understand, but it seems rude to say he doesn't. Somewhere in the back of his mind, which seems remarkably empty, he thinks maybe he has been hurrying too much. But when? He thinks maybe it was before he fell asleep on the other side of the world.

He looks at The Empress. She smiles at him, quite gently, he thinks. "Do you understand about love?" she asks. The Fool shakes his head. "What an ignorant person," says The Empress. "Everyone knows about love. Love is everywhere. Love is whatever you want it to be. Love is not being lonely. Love is remembering. Love is true—most of the time. Except when it's not. Do you understand?" the Empress asks. The Fool nods again, though he's not sure if he really does know anything— not just about love, whatever that is, but anything at all. Somewhere at the back of his remarkably empty mind, he thinks he remembers something, someone special to him, someone he wanted to be with all the time. Was that a problem?

He wants to ask The Empress, but she's not looking at him anymore. Neither is The Emperor. Now that he looks more closely, he sees they're made of stone, beautifully carved, but quite still and silent. He looks at The Enchantress, who is still standing by. He sees that she's smiling. "Did you learn anything?" she says. The Fool nods enthusiastically. "Good," she says. "Would you like to learn more?" The Fool nods again. "Good," she says again.

She turns away and produces a card that looks to The Fool a little bit like the cards The Magician in the town was playing with. This one shows a mysterious-looking man wrapped in a cloak. Not just any kind of cloak, but one made of mist. He walks out of the card and stands next to The Enchantress. They both look at The Fool, then at each other. The mist surrounds them all.

"Do you want to know who you were?" asks the mysterious man. The Fool thinks he knows but then thinks maybe he doesn't. Maybe I'm asleep, he wonders. Maybe this is a dream. He pinches himself to find out. Ouch! "If you want to know who you were, or who you are," says the mysterious man—whose name was The Hierophant, "you need to go on a journey. Do you want to do that?"

The Fool was thinking that he was already on a journey, so where would he go next? Then he realised that he didn't know where he was going or where he comes from, except that it was on the other side of the bridge made of a rainbow.

He shrugged and nodded. "Right, then," said The Hierophant. "Let's go."

The mist got very thick for a moment. It felt rather damp. Then The Fool found himself standing in another place. It was a very splendid palace: even more splendid than the one he had just been in. It had no coloured glass, but everything was painted all in red and white, with long drapes of those colours hanging from the ceiling. A small breeze blew, stirring the drapes, so that everything seemed to move and change all the time.

"This is the Palace of Love," said The Hierophant. "Watch and learn."

The Fool noticed that just in front of him was a stage. The kind of stage that actors walked on. And as he looked, some people came onto the stage, who he thought must be actors indeed. They began to walk up and down, waving their arms and declaiming loudly. At first The Fool wasn't sure about this, but gradually he realised that they were telling a story. Several stories, actually. The first story they told was about a great knight called Lancelot and a queen called Guinevere.

(iii)

There was once a king. He was called Arthur. The knight, Sir Lancelot, was the best of all (there were 150 knights who sat at a great Round Table). The king had a queen called Guinevere. He loved her very much. Sadly, the great knight fell in love with her as well. He tried to stay away—but couldn't. The king heard about the affair and got very angry. He started a war with Lancelot, and in the end another war began, and all the knights, and the king, died. The message seemed to be that love was dangerous and could do a lot of harm. The Fool tried to remember if he had ever been in love, or been loved, but he couldn't.

The next story was about a famous poet called Dante. He caught sight of a girl called Beatrice in the street. She was very young and liked going to church. He was quite old, but just seeing her made him feel so wonderful that he made a great poem about the light that he saw coming out of her. Then she died, and in his sorrow he wrote an even greater poem about

Heaven and Hell, and about waking up in the great dark forest of life.

The message this time seemed to The Fool to be that love could be very sad. He tried to remember if he had ever been sad because of being in love, but he couldn't remember that either. He thought maybe there was something like that at the back of his mind—but since that was remarkably empty, he did not have time to go and look for it. Instead he watched the actors telling the story of the Roman emperor Julius Caesar and his best friend, Anthony, both of whom fell in love with Cleopatra, the queen of Egypt. All three of them were very powerful and determined, but their love could not change the way the world works, so in the end the queen died of sorrow from the bite of a snake, Anthony died in battle, and Caesar was murdered by his friends, who were not friends at all.

This made The Fool think that the world in those days must have been a very sad place. Then he thought that maybe it still was—if only he could remember . . .

The next story was the saddest of all, about two young people called Romeo and Juliet. They loved each other very much, but in the end they both died. The Fool decided not to think too much about this one and parked it in the back of his very capacious and seemingly very empty mind. There was another story about some people called Troilus and Cressida, but by this time The Fool had stopped listening or watching. He had noticed something about the stage on which the actors were still walking around, waving their arms and shouting. The stage wasn't on land at all but floating on a sea that stretched away into the distance. As he was still watching it began to float away, until finally all he could see were the actors waving their arms in the air, though he couldn't tell whether they were still acting or waving because they wanted someone to come and rescue them from the sea.

While he was looking on, a rumbling sound came to his ears, and when he looked round, he saw a huge Chariot racing toward him, the rims of its wheels striking sparks from the ground. It was pulled by two huge white horses, whose breath was like smoke and who were constantly trying to go in opposite directions from each other. The Chariot was driven by a very tall, very powerful-looking man with flame-red hair, who shouted at the horses and pulled on the reins all the time. He drew up right next to The Fool and invited him, with a big booming voice, to get in. The Fool looked around and couldn't see any of the people who'd been there before, not even the little dog, so he thought, "Why not?" and got into The Chariot.

Immediately the very tall man shook the reins and the two white horses sped off as fast as they could. They went faster than breath. So fast that The Fool was fairly sure they actually took off and flew through the air. But as he had both eyes tightly closed, he couldn't be sure. Quite soon after, The Chariot came to a halt. The charioteer picked up The Fool by the scruff of his neck and dumped him back on the ground. Then he rode off, laughing a great booming laugh, and finally taking off entirely, so that The Fool knew they must really have been flying before.

(iv)

Where they had landed, the path branched in three directions. All of them looked the same. Which one should he take? As he stood there, the little dog came in sight, barking delightedly. Immediately it raced away down the middle path.

The Fool followed the dog until he came to a place where the land rose and became a rocky valley. He was listening for the dog, whom he thought must be nearby, but instead of barking he heard a loud roaring noise. He rounded some rocks, and there in front of him was a tall, willowy lady dressed in green. In front of her was a great golden lion. It was this that was doing the roaring. The Fool stopped dead in his tracks, but the Lady didn't seem at all worried. She said something to the lion, which The Fool couldn't hear, then she leaned forward and, taking the lion's head between her hands, opened its jaws and bent her head to look inside. Whatever it was she saw seemed to satisfy her, because she let go of the lion's head and patted it instead. Then she scratched between its ears and instead of roaring it began to purr. It sounded like a cat but much louder. The Fool took a step closer. The lion looked up and shook its great mane. It started to growl, but the Lady smiled and rested her hand on its head.

"Hello, Fool," she said. "I am Strength." "You must be very strong," said The Fool, looking at the lion. The Lady laughed. "I am," she said. "But Strength comes from love as well as muscles. If you or I wrestled with this mighty beast, we would probably get eaten. But I have seen into its heart, and I can tell it does not want to fight with me." The Fool thought this was something very special, though he wasn't sure how. Strength looked at him and said, "You'll need lots of Strength in the future. But don't depend on that alone. Everything counts, you know." The Fool frowned. He wanted to ask what "everything" was, but he was too shy. So he thanked the Lady, who waved him on his way.

As soon as he turned the next corner in the valley, he found the little dog waiting. It was very glad to see him, and he it. Together they followed the road until they came to a place where there was a small hole in the rocks. A small plume of smoke came from it, and a lovely cooking smell. The Fool's mouth began to water. He walked up to the hole and stuck his head through it. Inside was a small cave, and there sat a small man cooking something over a fire. At first, he didn't even look up but simply said, "Go away!" The Fool hesitated. He didn't want to annoy the man, but he was very hungry. "Excuse me," said The Fool. "I don't want to bother you, but your cooking smells so good . . ." The man looked up. He had a great beard and very bright-blue eyes. "Well, you'd better come in then," he said.

The Fool entered the cave and sat down next to the man, who said nothing at all for quite a long time. Soon the food was ready, and the man put some onto a plate for himself and onto another plate for The Fool. Neither of them said anything for a bit, as they were too busy chewing. "Thank you," said The Fool when he had eaten every scrap of food on his plate. The man nodded. He looked at The Fool for a while, then he said: "I don't see many people. Actually I don't want to see anyone. I came here to be alone and think."

"I'm sorry if I disturbed you," said The Fool.

"That's all right," said the man. "Thinking is very useful at times, and I have plenty of time to read and think."

"You must be very clever then," said The Fool.

"Not at all," said the man. "Just thinking isn't enough to make anyone clever. It's what happens when you put all the words and thoughts together that's important. Sometimes you can make something new out of them—even if they are old. People say that all the best and wisest things have already been said, but I'm not sure. That's why I came here to try to find out if it's true or not."

The Fool looked at him. "Do you know anything about me?" he asked. "I think you've come a long way," answered the man. "And I think you still have a long way to go. The big question is, are you dreaming or are you awake?"

"That's what I was wondering," said The Fool.

"Well, keep thinking," said the man. "I've been a Hermit for a long time, and I still haven't found any answers. But I believe there are answers to be found, so I'm going to keep looking. If you want my advice, you'll do the same. Goodbye now."

He said nothing more, so The Fool stood up and thanked the man for the food and his words and left the cave. Outside he found the dog sitting in the sun, with its tongue hanging out. Immediately, it jumped up and ran around him in circles, barking madly. The Fool was getting quite used to this by now, so he laughed at the dog and off they went again.

(v)

They went on for a long while, until The Fool began to feel sleepy. He tried to remember the last time he had slept, but couldn't. So when he saw a shady hollow just ahead, he went and lay down. The little dog came and lay next to him, and soon they were both sleeping. The Fool dreamed. Until now he had no idea that it was possible to have a dream while you were already in a dream. Or maybe he wasn't—maybe he was awake all the time? Or maybe he was awake when he thought he was dreaming, and the hut and everything about it was a dream? In the dream—if dream it was—he saw a giant Wheel, so tall that three or four Fools could have stood on each other's heads and still not reached the top. As he looked, he saw that there were several people on The Wheel. They sat in chairs, which somehow stopped them falling off, because The Wheel turned all the time, so that sometimes the person at the top was at the bottom, which meant that the person who was at the bottom was then at the top. The ones in between took turns at being either the top or the bottom. The Fool found this very strange indeed, but at that moment along came The Enchantress, whom he had met earlier.

She asked The Fool what he thought about The Wheel. The Fool looked at it for a while and then said that maybe it meant that people who were at the top didn't stay there all the time but could actually end up on the bottom. The Enchantress smiled. "You're not really such a foolish Fool, are you?" she said. "If you like, you could get onto The Wheel and see where you will go. The Fool thought for a moment, then he climbed up onto The Wheel and sat in the middle on the hub. That way, The Wheel kept turning but he stayed in the same place.

The Fool smiled, and The Enchantress couldn't stop laughing. Then she stood very tall and raised her arms and waved them at The Fool. At that moment a huge bird, the largest he'd ever seen in his life—or at least that he could re-member seeing—flew down and picked him up. It flew very fast and very high, with The Fool dangling from its big, clawed feet. The Fool laughed out loud at this. It was the best thing ever that he could remember.

All too soon the journey was over. The bird flew down and dropped The Fool at the entrance to a small grove of trees. Then it flew off, leaving The Fool wondering what was going to happen next.

The road wound around and around until it left the valley

behind; there in front of them was the sparking sea. The little dog began to bark at once and rushed, jumping into the water. The Fool watched it for a while, then he caught sight of something moving out at sea. At first he thought it was a ship floating out on the sea, but as it got closer he saw that it was the stage on which the actors had been telling the stories of love.

The Fool waded out into the sea, which felt quite warm, and very soon he was standing on the edge of the floating stage. At first he found it difficult to understand what story it was that the actors were telling this time. Then he saw one of them standing at the side who didn't seem to be taking part at all, or maybe just hadn't gotten to his place in the play yet.

"Excuse me," said The Fool. "What story are you telling?"

The actor looked down at him and spoke in his big booming voice: "Why, we're telling the story of the Goddess with the Scales," he said.

The Fool saw that one the actors was holding aloft a huge set of scales. One of them pointed to him and beckoned, and the actor he'd spoken to said, "Go on, you have to get weighed!"

So now The Fool was in the play. He went forward cautiously, and when he got to the middle of the floating stage, he found that it wasn't one of the actors anymore who was holding the scales, but a very beautiful woman, with a crown on her head, which looked as though it might have been made of stars. And when she looked at him, he thought that her eyes looked like stars as well, and he found that he couldn't really look at her directly.

The beautiful woman, who was really a goddess, suddenly became very tall. And with one hand she lifted up The Fool and placed him into one of the bowls of the scale. The Fool expected that the scales would tip down on his side with his weight, but instead he found himself going up into the air, until he was at the same height as the Goddess's face. By now he was feeling a little afraid, because after all this was a goddess, and he had never met one before as far as he knew. Then he wondered how it was that he knew she was one if he'd never seen one before.

"I believe you have a question," said the Goddess.

"Please," said The Fool. "I've been travelling for a long time. And I think I need to know who I am, or who I was, or who I will be?"

"Those are very big questions," said the Goddess. "But they are also very good questions . . . let me see now . . ." She put out a hand and spun The Fool around and around and around as if he weighed nothing at all. The Fool shut his eyes. He began to feel quite dizzy and didn't know what was happening.

After a while he stopped whirling, but in his head it still felt as if he was spinning. Slowly, he opened his eyes. He was standing at the entrance to a small patch of woodland. The little dog was there and raced ahead as usual until it vanished amid the trees. The Fool followed and came to a place where the trees stood in a circle. Each one was a different colour. The Fool could not remember ever having seen anything like this before, so he walked around the circle, touching the trunk of each tree. When he did so, it seemed that he heard a sound like music. Just a small shining note that sounded as though it might be part of a much bigger piece of music. The last tree in the circle was very dark, and when he touched the trunk, the sound he heard was more like a groan, and a noose suddenly pulled tight around his ankle. The next minute, he found himself hanging upside down in the air. Strangely, this made The Fool feel happy. He continued to hang upside down in the tree, laughing as hard as he could, until a strange-looking man came in sight.

The man was dressed in ragged clothes that had definitely seen better days, and over his shoulder he carried a big scythe, which looked as if it had been sharpened recently. He stood at the bottom of the tree and looked up at The Fool. His face was weathered like old leather, but his eyes were bright and sharp.

"That looks like an uncomfortable place to be," he said. "But you seem to be enjoying it."

"It's funny seeing everything upside down," said The Fool. "It makes everything look different."

"Ah," said the man. "You're not the first person to have said that. Do you want to come down?"

The Fool thought for a moment. "Yes, please," he said.

The man swung the scythe and The Fool tumbled down onto the ground. He sat there thinking that now things looked different right way up. The man look down at him and said, "My name is Mr. Death. You don't know me yet, but there will come a time when I'll be your best friend."

The Fool didn't know what to make of this, but the weathered man reached out a hand to help him up, and when he grasped it, it felt very cold, and suddenly everything went very blurry again, and The Fool fell asleep—though once again he wasn't sure whether he was in a dream and falling awake, or awake and falling into a dream.

The Fool heard the sound of a stream gurgling along. He opened his eyes and saw that he was lying in the middle a soft green meadow. A small stream was indeed rushing by, and as he stood up, The Fool saw that it flowed into a wider stretch of water that was more like a river. Sitting on a rock at the exact place where the two streams of water met was a woman. The Fool looked at her long golden hair, which flowed around her as if it was itself water, and saw that she was very beautiful indeed. He thought to himself that he had seen several lovely ladies on his journey so far, and that this was surely a good thing. He looked at what she was doing, and saw that she was scooping up water from the stream and emptying it into the river.

At first The Fool thought this was a strange thing to do, but then he noticed that when the water from the stream went into the vessel The Lady was holding, it was just plain water, but that when it came out and went into the river, it was a different colour—though The Fool wasn't quite sure that he could tell what colour it was.

Without looking up from what she was doing, The Lady said: "Water is never the same twice. It changes all the time. Life is a bit like that, don't you think? Everywhere on your journey there have been choices: Which way to go? What to do? Sometimes your friend the little dog has helped show you the way; sometimes you worked it out for yourself. I won't say if they were always good choices, but they were usually interesting, don't you think?"

The Fool nodded.

"It's all about balance, you see," said The Lady. "If you get the balance right, if the water flows properly, everything feels better. And if it feels better, it usually is better. And sometimes it feels more than better—don't you think?"

The Fool thought about this and nodded again. If he was absolutely honest, he didn't know if this was really true, but it felt right.

As if she had heard this thought, The Lady stopped what she was doing for a moment and offered The Fool a drink from her vessel. Suddenly he thought he had never been more thirsty in all his life, and he tried not to snatch the proffered drink too quickly, or to drink it all at once. The water tasted more wonderful than anything he'd ever tasted in his whole life—at least as much as he could remember. When he had drunk every last drop, he gave it back to The Lady—whose name was Temperance—who carried on dipping it into the water and pouring it into the river and watching it change color.

The Fool realised that he was getting very sleepy again, and the wonderful green meadow seemed so attractive to him that he couldn't help just lying down there, and in a moment he was fast asleep.

(vii)

It was probably the best sleep that The Fool ever had. At least it felt like that when he woke up. The strange thing was that he was no longer lying in the soft green meadow but in a very different place. A rather wild place, where neither trees nor bushes grew, water definitely did not run, and where a cold wind seemed to blow all the time.

Coming toward him across this unfriendly-looking place was a very unfriendly-looking person. At first The Fool thought

171

he was wearing a strange costume, but as he got nearer, he saw that this was not the case. The person, or creature, whichever it was, was covered in scales. Shiny bright scales that glittered in the rather dull light of the place. His, or its, head seemed like a strange shape, long and narrow rather than round as most human heads were. This strange person stopped in front of him and opened its mouth. The Fool had a good look at a lot of very sharp teeth. When he looked a bit closer, he saw that the being seemed to have a tail, also covered in scales and with sharp ridges all the way down to the tip, which was barbed like a spear. In fact, it looked like nothing so much as a dragon, except that it walked upright on its feet and had arms and hands. It also had horns, which curved like swords out of its head and made it look even more fierce.

The Fool thought about running away, but before he could, the creature seized him in its big, taloned hands and tossed him over its shoulder like a bundle of old clothes. The Fool wondered if he should ask this strange creature what it wanted with him, but he didn't, thinking that maybe it would say, "Supper." So he kept quiet.

The strange Dragon-Man walked across the dry, dusty landscape at a good pace until finally he reached his destination and set The Fool down on the ground. They had come to a round, tall tower, built of huge blocks of stone. It had one narrow door. The Dragon-Man went through the door, pushing The Fool ahead of him. Inside it was mostly dark, but there was just enough light to see where a flight of worn stone steps curved away round the inside of the wall. Up the Dragon-Man went, pushing The Fool ahead of him. Finally they reached another door, which the Dragon opened, and pushed The Fool through into a small room. The door closed with a bang, leaving The Fool standing in a small stone chamber with one window. He went straight to the window and looked out. All he could see into the distance was the dusty plain across which they had come. There were no rivers or streams, no trees or bushes, just dust and dryness.

How long he stayed there, The Fool could not tell. He realised that he had not thought once about time, how much he had spent in this strange world, full of musical trees, strange magicians, enchantresses, and huge birds. The more he thought about it, the more he believed that this must be a dream. But if it was a dream, it was the most real one he'd ever experienced. Once again, he pinched himself to see if he could wake up. He didn't. Ouch!

While he was thinking about this, The Fool realised that The Tower was beginning to shake. He thought it must be an earthquake. Everything shook, including The Fool. Then The Tower just fell down. There were no two ways about it; that was what happened. One moment The Tower was standing, dark and grim, and next it was a heap of dust. Amazingly, The Fool was not hurt at all. He simply found himself standing in the middle of broken stones and dust. For some reason, he remembered what a wise man once told him: that dust was actually very magical and probably had a lot to do with the way the universe was made.

Maybe it was this thought that caused the next thing to happen—because suddenly The Fool found that he was flying through the air—not clutched in the claws of a giant bird this time, but just flying, and as he flew, the light began to dim, until it was almost dark, and looking up above him he saw the whole great dome of the heavens picked out with stars. The Fool thought this was the most beautiful thing he had ever seen, though of course there might have been other things just as beautiful in the world he once lived in.

Higher and higher he flew, and now he was looking down at the earth below him and seeing the great round pebble of the planet. And while he was looking at that, and getting more full of wonder every moment, he realised that everything was getting lighter. He looked up and saw a hole in the sky, through which the light shone. Before he had time to wonder what this was, he flew through the hole and found himself in another place.

(viii)

The place seemed made of light, so that The Fool couldn't really see anything of what was around him—if indeed there was anything. Then he noticed something strange. He looked down at his hands and found that he could see right through them. Then he looked at as much of his body as he could see, and found that that too was becoming transparent. How on earth—or in the sky—would anyone be able to see him ever again if he stayed like this?

While he was thinking about this, he heard quiet laughter and realised that he wasn't alone anymore. Standing before him was the most beautiful person he had ever seen in his entire life (at least as far as he could remember). This beautiful being was neither man nor woman, though it could have been either. It shone with light so bright that The Fool almost had to close his eyes. Into his head came the thought that he was looking at a Star.

"Why are you here?" asked The Star. "Hardly anyone ever comes here."

The Fool thought about this question and suddenly found that he was telling The Star all about his journey—about the little dog and the rainbow bridge and The Magician, and The Enchantress. He talked about The Emperor of Time and The Empress of Love, and how The Hierophant had taken him to the Palace of Love, with its red-and-white drapes. And he tried to remember the plays and stories that he'd seen—about great romances, most of which seemed to have sad endings. Then he told about being carried off by the bird and landing in the forest and ending up hanging upside down, and how Mr. Death came and set him free. And how he ate a wonderful meal in the little house made of leaves and flowers and twigs and how The Enchantress showed him the great wheel.

All these things and everything else he told The Star, right up to the moment when The Tower fell, and he flew through the air and came through the hole in the sky and there he was. And all of this The Star listened to with amazement. And at the end, all she could say was "That's the most amazing story I've ever heard. And I promise you I have heard very many."

The Star asked him how this had all come about. The Fool said, "I'm really not sure, but I think it's to do with my quest." "What quest is that?" asked The Star. And The Fool, who had not thought he was on any kind of quest until that moment, answered, "I think I'm trying to find out who I am, or who I was, or who I will be." Then he looked shyly at The Star and said, "Can you tell me?"

The Star looked thoughtful for a while, then said, "That's too hard a question for me, but maybe my sister The Moon can tell you. Would you like to ask her?"

The Fool nodded eagerly, and the next moment there was a swirling motion in the air, and he found himself falling back down, down, and down through the hole in the sky, under the light of The Star, until he landed standing on top of a mountain. And he realised it was nighttime, and that he was back on the earth, and above him shining in the sky was the great round Moon.

The Fool looked up at The Moon and wondered how he was going to talk to her. She was rather a long way away, and he thought that even if he shouted, she would not hear. Then once again he heard the little dog barking, and when he looked, he saw a tall and very beautiful lady coming toward him. She was clad all in blue, and there was a shimmeringness and shiningness about her that told him she was The Moon.

The nearer she got, the more shy The Fool felt. But when she came right up to him, suddenly his shyness fell away, because in the presence of The Moon he felt more comfortable than he had ever felt in his whole life—or at least the part he could remember, which was, of course, not very much.

"So you are The Fool that everyone is talking about," said The Moon.

"Are they?" answered The Fool, amazed.

The Moon nodded. "I hear from my sister that you have a question to ask me?"

"If it's all right," said The Fool. He took a deep breath. "I've been travelling for a long time. In fact, I'm not sure how long I've been travelling, or even if I'm really travelling or if this is just a dream. But I really want to know who I am, or who I was, or who I will be."

"That sounds like three questions to me," said The Moon, but she was smiling as she said it, so The Fool knew she wasn't angry.

The Moon thought for a while, then she shook her head.

176

"I'm sorry," she said, "but that's really too hard a question or three for me. I think you should go and ask my brother The Sun."

And while The Fool was still thinking about this, The Moon waved her hand and The Fool felt himself lifted up and carried very fast through the air, so fast that the night turned to day in a few seconds, and he found himself walking along the shore of a great sea. Then suddenly there was a lot of very bright light, and The Fool saw a man walking ahead of him along the sand. The Fool noticed at once that he had flaming red hair, and recognised him as the same man who had driven The Chariot in an earlier part of his journey.

"Excuse me," said The Fool. The man with the flaming red hair, whom The Fool guessed must be The Sun, stopped and turned around. His eyes were so bright that The Fool almost had to shade his. The Sun spoke in a big booming voice, for indeed everything about him seemed large and loud.

"My sister The Moon says you want to know some very complicated things," said The Sun.

"Yes, please," said The Fool. And he repeated his questions.

The Sun smiled at him, and The Fool couldn't help noticing how bright his teeth were. "Those are very hard questions indeed," said The Sun. "I have a feeling they mean you are almost at the end of your journey." He thought for a moment, then said, "I think you need to ask The Lady Judgement."

The Sun pointed to where a stone building stood, a little way off. Something about it made The Fool feel uncomfortable, but since all the great beings of the heavens had been kind to him, he decided to go where The Sun told him to.

When he reached the building, The Fool saw that it had two great doors, on which were carved all kinds of strange symbols. Tentatively he raised a hand to knock on the door, and at once it swung open. Inside it was cool and shadowy. The Fool walked forward and found that he needed to tiptoe, because somehow this seemed like a place where one should not make noise. The little dog was nowhere to be seen, which was just as well, considering a need for quiet.

The Fool walked on into the building, which turned out to have just one big room, with tall stone pillars on every side. He thought it reminded him of the palace of The Emperor of Time and The Empress of Love. Right at the far end he saw a tall chair that seemed more like a throne. In it sat a Lady with a very stern face, though The Fool thought her eyes were kind.

When The Fool stood in front of her, he found that he felt very small indeed, and that he did not know what to say. After a moment, The Lady said, "Why have you come?" She said it quite gently, and The Fool found that suddenly he could speak.

"I've been on a really long journey," he said. "I think I've been trying to find out who I am, or who I was, or even who I will be. Can you help?"

The Lady in the chair looked down at him and said, "I think it's probably time for you to wake up."

"Oh!" said The Fool, "I've been wondering if I was asleep all this time."

"There is more than one kind of sleep," said The Lady. "Sometimes it's hard to judge which is which."

"I'm not sure I know how to wake up—if I am asleep," said The Fool.

"I think the answer is probably outside," said The Lady in the chair. "That's my judgement anyway. It's time to begin again."

(ix)

With the words of the wise Lady ringing in his head, The Fool turned around and walked back outside. He found that he was somewhere that looked strangely familiar. Then he realised it was the place where he had first woken up at the start of his journey, no longer knowing who he was.

Looking around him, the first thing he sees is the little dog, which was, as usual, dancing and spinning and barking with delight. The next thing The Fool sees is a bridge that seems to be made out of a rainbow and stretches between the place where he is and a fair green country on the other side. The Fool thinks there is something really familiar about this too, but he can't remember exactly why.

"What should I do?" asks The Fool, out loud. The dog begins to bark even more wildly than before and dances around The Fool until he begins to feel quite dizzy again. Then The Fool hears a sound behind him and sees a group of people coming toward him. He realises they are some of the people he met on his journey. There is The Magician, The Enchantress, The Hierophant, Strength, and The Hermit, and all the rest. Even Mr. Death is there, smiling, with his great scythe, and next to him is the Dragon-Man, who grins rather wolfishly. Then there is The Star, The Moon, and The Sun. All of them are smiling and waving.

The Fool doesn't know what to do, but he feels very happy to see all his old friends again—even the ones who were not so friendly. One by one they come up to him, and every one of them has something to give him. The Magician gives him a new pair of shoes, for his old ones are much worn. The Enchantress gives him a cloak to keep out the rain. The

Hierophant gives him a big key that would open any door, and The Hermit a lantern with which to see the way. Mr. Death says, "Remember me," before dissolving into mist. The Dragon-Man gives him a knife and fork, both of which seem very blunt, but he says nothing, so The Fool is not sure what they are for. Strength gives him . . . well . . . strength; The Star gives him courage, The Sun gives him hope, and The Moon gifts him with the ability to dream true. Last of all comes Temperance, still carrying her vessel from which a little fresh stream of water runs all the time. She gives him a little box. The Fool opens it. Inside is a pack of cards. The first one is called The Fool, and the picture on it looks just like him.

"It's time for you to go on," chorus all the people he has met on his journey. "Only by seeking the truth, in whatever form it comes, will you find out who you were, who you are, and who you are meant to be. The World is waiting for you!"

The Fool looks at the pack of cards. The figures seem to be moving somehow, and the more he looks, the more he sees different things happening. Suddenly, they don't look anything like his journey, though the people look the same.

The Fool begins to laugh . . . and as he does so he wakes up and finds that he's sitting in the middle of a great field of golden wheat. The sun is shining; he has new shoes, a new cloak, a key and a lantern, and a knife and fork; and in his hands is a pack of cards.

"Was it all a dream?" he asks himself.

He hears a dog barking.

THE FOOL'S NEW JOURNEY

(A Tarot Fable)

He's back again, the same old Fool but in a new suit of clothes. Still looking for the way home, still hungry for wisdom and knowledge, still uncertain which is which and what is what. Let's follow him and see where this new journey takes him, on paths old and familiar, but mostly new, something his poor old head can hardly understand.

(i)

He wakes again, The Fool, wondering if this is home. It's not, he thinks. At least it's nothing like he expects (*but then*, he wonders, *What do I expect?*). He's standing in front of a high wall in which a single narrow door offers a way in. The Fool hesitates. He's been here before—well, not here as such, but offered entrances and exits to places he wasn't sure he wanted to go into or come out of.

Cautiously he sticks his head through the entrance. In front is another wall, but to either side are open ways—narrow passages that lead out of sight, all of them open to the sky. There's no one there but him, so he steps into the passageway, automatically turning left, because that's what he always does, and follows the path until the passage turns right, then left, then right, then left . . . and so on.

All the passages look exactly the same. Bricks on bricks, just too high for him to see over. They twist and turn, each one leading farther in.

After a while, The Fool realises he's in a Maze. He thinks perhaps he's been in one before—following a path that seems to lead nowhere but actually leads somewhere. He vaguely remembers another journey he took—he's not sure when—that seemed to wander on and on. He still has a bag of things that he came back with from that journey, and that he carries on his back. Inside is a big key, a knife and fork, and a small deck of cards, which he thinks tell a story that he once knew but has since forgotten.

He's not sure how long he keeps walking in The Maze, but eventually he comes to what he thinks is the centre. It's a big round space, with several exits and entrances, including the one he came in by. In the middle is a fountain that shoots up into the air and falls into a round basin.

Sitting by the fountain is a woman. She's dressed in a white suit and has a very pleasant face (The Believer).

"Do you believe?" she asks The Fool.

"Believe in what?" The Fool inquires.

"Well—yourself, for instance," says the woman.

"I'm not sure," says The Fool, thoughtfully.

"Well you should," says the woman, still smiling. "How else will you know who you are?"

"Funny you should say that," The Fool says. "I think that's why I'm here. To find out who I am, or who I was. Even who I will be."

"Ah," says the woman. "Well, you need to believe you know what's going on first. If you don't you start to forget everything."

"But what if I don't want to believe?" says The Fool.

"That's up to you," the woman answers. "No one should try to persuade you if something is true or not. Only you can do that."

While The Fool is thinking this over, the woman takes a little silver cup out of her pocket and fills it with water from the fountain. First, she takes a drink for herself, then refills the cup and offers it to The Fool.

"This will help you remember," she says. *Remember what?* The Fool wonders, but he takes the cup politely and drinks. The water tastes wonderfully fresh and cold, but almost immediately The Fool begins to feel sleepy. He hopes he hasn't been poisoned. Next minute he's asleep, and (maybe) begins to dream.

(ii)

Whether he's awake or asleep, The Fool feels rather gloomy. He thinks he was supposed to remember something, but he can't remember what. He looks around and finds he's on a road leading down from a high place into a wide valley. He sees some houses down there and decides to go in that direction. The sun is shining overhead, and after a while The Fool notices something strange. His Shadow is behaving really oddly. Instead of echoing everything he does, it does something different. Just to test it, The Fool tries a few skipping steps, jumping in the air, and landing on the ground. His shadow runs in circles. Next, The Fool tries waving his arms, but when he does his Shadow points to both left and right. The Fool slows right down and comes to a stop. His Shadow keeps on going for a bit, then stops and turns back.

"Now look," says The Fool. "You're my Shadow and you ought to do the same things I do."

"Why should I?" answers The Shadow.

"Because I want you to," says The Fool.

"No one can have everything they want," answers The Shadow.

"This is silly," says The Fool.

"I disagree," answers The Shadow. "Sometimes when you're happy, I feel sad, so why should I have to make happy shadows when in fact I want to make sad ones?"

"When you put it like that," says The Fool, "I'm not sure."

"Exactly," says The Shadow. "You should remember that in the future if we're going to get along."

"I'll try to," says The Fool. He goes marching on down the road, and after a while his Shadow falls in beside him and copies everything he does.

Soon, The Fool reaches the village that he'd seen from the higher place. It's just a handful of houses, and there's no one to be seen until he reaches the square in the middle. There he sees a table set up. Standing behind it is a man in a top hat (The Magician). He seems vaguely familiar. The Fool walks over to say hello and sees that the man is laying out cards on the table. He keeps turning them over, and shuffling them about, so that they never really stop moving.

"Have we met before?" asks The Fool. The man does not answer but keeps on shuffling the cards. Then The Fool notices something really strange about him. He doesn't just have two arms, like everyone else, but four. And while two of his arms are shuffling the pack of cards on the table, the other two are shuffling a second pack behind his back.

This makes The Fool feel very strange, and since the man in the top hat doesn't seem to want to talk to him, The Fool carries on. He soon leaves the village behind and is back on the road. Ahead he sees a little house, with a very tidy garden in front of it, and a little white gate opening onto a path that leads up to the front door. The Fool decides to go and ask for directions, though he's not sure where to. He walks up the path and sees that the door has an old-fashioned-looking brass knocker on it. It looks like a frowning face—not frowning angrily, but as if deep in thought.

The Fool knocks on the door. After a moment, it's opened by a very finely dressed lady (The Priestess). She wears a strange hat that makes him think it's a kind of crown. "Come in," says the lady, smiling at him. "Sit and have some tea."

The Fool does as he's asked. The table is already laden with sandwiches, cakes, and tea. The Fool sits down, and the lady takes her place opposite.

"Have we met before?" asks The Fool.

The lady looks at him. "Oh yes," she says. "Several times."

"I thought you looked familiar," says The Fool, "but I'm sorry I can't remember where we met."

"That's because it was a long way away and probably a long time ago," says the lady. "I'm The Priestess, and once upon a time I helped you, when you were lost."

"I'm afraid I'm still a bit lost," says The Fool.

"I can see that," says The Priestess. "What are we going to do about it?"

The Fool can't think of anything to say, so he helps himself to a sandwich and munches in silence. The Priestess pours two cups of tea, then she smiles. "I think you have to learn about things that nearly everyone has forgotten. They are still very important, and a few of us keep them alive."

"What kind of things?" asks The Fool.

"Old ways of doing things," replies The Priestess. "They are called traditions (The Tradition). I have three friends I want you to meet. In fact, you've met them all before, though you won't remember because it was a long time ago and in another place. But they have things to tell you that will help you on your way. Finish up your tea and we'll go."

The Fool finishes up his sandwiches and cakes and drinks several more cups of tea. Then The Priestess stands up and opens a little door, which The Fool could have sworn was not there moments before. "Come," she says. "Follow me."

(iii)

The Fool expected to go into another part of the house, but instead he found himself in a big, airy room with long windows through which the sun shone long beams of golden light. At the far end of the room were two thrones, and in them sat two very powerful-looking people. Both wore elaborate crowns and were dressed in rich clothing.

"Let me introduce you," said The Priestess. "This is The Empress of Ancient Wisdom, though most people just call her The Empress. And this is The Emperor of Timeless Wisdom."

The Fool stood before the two august people and could not think of anything to say. He thought they both looked a little sad, but they smiled at him nonetheless, and The Empress asked, "Do you know about the Ancient Wisdom?"

"I'm afraid I don't. Or at least I don't think so," answered The Fool. "I suppose it must be very old."

"Older than time itself," said The Emperor. "Nowadays people have mostly forgotten about these things. But they should remember—because older times still have a lot to teach us."

"What kind of things?" asked The Fool.

"How to be, and how to see, how to understand the patterns

186

in things," said The Empress. The Emperor nodded. "How to do and ask and remember the answers," he said. "Too many people have forgotten how to do these things."

The Fool thought there was a note of sadness in The Emperor's words.

"How can we learn to remember these things?" The Fool asked.

"By taking journeys like the one you are taking," answered The Empress. "One day, if they don't, The Emperor and I will cease to exist."

"How can I help?" The Fool asked. "I'm not very clever."

"You're a lot cleverer than you think," said The Priestess. "As I told you once before—you are not such a foolish Fool."

"There is one thing you can do," said The Emperor. "Continue with your journey and pay attention to all that you see and hear. Look and listen, and above all, remember . . . then, when you get to the end, tell your story to as many people as you can. If they do the same, the word will spread. Tradition will not die but keep on growing and changing. People will realise that older things still have a lot to tell them. They will remember how to be again."

The Fool stood up as straight and tall as he could. "I'll do that," he declared. "If I can . . . ?"

"Of course you can," said The Priestess. Let's go and meet another old friend. He will show you the best way to do what you've promised to do."

The Fool said goodbye to The Emperor and Empress, both of whom smiled and wished him well. He thought perhaps they looked less sad than they had before, and he felt really determined to help. *Maybe the journey is not just about me,* he thought. *Maybe others can learn from what I see.*

"Quite right," said The Priestess, as though she had heard what The Fool was thinking. "Quite right."

She led the way out of the big hall and into a small side room, which had a second door that was firmly closed and locked. "'I think you may already have what you need to open the door," said The Priestess.

The Fool thought for a moment, then remembered that the things in his pack included a big key. Quickly he rummaged for it and inserted it into the lock on the door. It fitted perfectly and turned easily. The door swung open, and The Fool entered another chamber. A man was sitting at a desk, reading a great book. He looked up and smiled at The Fool.

"How good it is to see you again," he said.

"Have we met before?" asked The Fool.

"Oh yes," said the man. "I am The Hierophant. We met on another journey you took, before this one. It was I who gave you the key to this room."

"I'm sorry," answered The Fool. "I really don't remember anything about that journey."

"That's a pity," said The Hierophant. "I think you learned a lot of helpful things. But never mind. Maybe if you finish this journey, you'll remember the other one." He paused, seeming to look into the distance as if he saw things The Fool did not. "Now," he said. "What can I do for you today?"

"Well," said The Fool. "I want to help The Empress and The Emperor spread the word about the old ways and how they can help people now. But I don't really know much about them."

"I see," said The Hierophant. "Hmmm. The first thing you need to know about is Wonder. Let me show you."

He turned a few pages in the great book he had been

studying, then turned it around so that The Fool could see what was on the page. "Here we are. Come and look."

The Fool stepped forward and looked at the book. The pages were very brown and crinkled with age, but in the middle of the page he was looking at was a picture showing a young woman looking at a small figure that seemed to dance and shimmer between her hands. She was wide eyed and seemed to be unaware of anything else.

The Fool looked closer and realised this was not just a picture but a living person. As he leaned closer, he suddenly found himself falling forward. The next moment, he was in the room where the young woman sat. She didn't even notice him at all but kept looking at the small figure between her hands as if it was something very important that needed to be kept safe.

"Excuse me," said The Fool. The girl started and looked at him wide eyed.

"What do you want?" she asked.

"I was just wondering," said The Fool, "what you were doing?"

"Oh," said the girl, "I'm looking after Wonder."

"What exactly is wonder?" asked The Fool.

The girl looked at him. "Do you really not know?" she said.

"Well, I know what wonder is, I suppose, but I've never seen it like that before," said The Fool, looking at the small figure the girl had been watching so intently.

The girl sat back on her heels and stared at him. "Wonder is everywhere," she said. "It's everything that matters. This is just a tiny piece of it," she added, indicating the little figure.

The Fool looked more closely and saw that it looked like

a statue of a human being, but very simple and unadorned. It didn't even seem to have a face. But as he looked at it, The Fool felt a curious sensation coming over him. Into his mind came everything he could remember that had been wonderful, magical, and beautiful. So wonderful these seemed that he gasped aloud.

The girl smiled. "Now do you see?" she said

The Fool nodded. "Everything is wonderful," he said. "Even the things you think are not."

"Exactly," said the girl. "Now you understand. You need to look at everything again. Why not start here?" She pointed to a window, which The Fool had not noticed before. He went over to it and looked out. What he saw was indeed wonderful.

(iv)

The Fool saw a staircase that disappeared into misty clouds. Coming down the stairs was a person (Beauty). The Fool couldn't tell if it was a man or a woman, an adult or a child, and that didn't matter. What he did know straight away was that it was beautiful. More beautiful perhaps than anything he had ever seen in all his life—at least as far as he could remember. His heart began to beat faster, and he felt a big smile spreading over his face. For a moment he thought he heard the girl laughing delightedly in the room behind him, but The Fool wasn't interested in that any longer; he just wanted to get closer to the beautiful being that he saw on the stairs.

Quick as thought, he jumped through the window out into what seemed like a landscape made of clouds. Surprisingly, The Fool did not fall through them but was able to walk on the clouds. They were soft and bouncy like a feather bed he remembered seeing—though he couldn't remember where. But however much he looked, he could see no sign of the beautiful being he had seen from the window. Instead, he found himself looking at two people walking side by side, hand in hand, across the cloudy landscape (Lovers). As he watched, they walked on for a little way, then stopped. They seemed to be looking out at something The Fool couldn't see. Then he saw them put their arms around each other and cling together. He couldn't tell for sure, but he thought maybe they were afraid, and then from somewhere came the thought of stories he'd been told about love and how dangerous it could be, as well as how wonderful. But the two people were very clearly in love, and The Fool thought he remembered how that felt, and how comforting it was as well.

He thought about the perfect being he had seen on the stairs, and wondered if it wasn't love he had felt when he first caught sight of it. Perhaps the people he saw ahead of him could tell him?

The Fool set off in their direction, but something happened that he could not understand. As he got closer to the couple, the lovely cloudy landscape changed, until he found himself looking out at a very different place. Just as the clouds were light and fluffy, so the world he looked out on now was hard, dark grey, and grim. Everywhere he looked he saw broken trees, dead grass, earth churned up and dried and cracked. He felt a terrible sense of loss, as though in this desolate place, where nothing seemed to grow, his own life became dull and meaningless. Somehow, he knew that this was somewhere he had been before, and the name for it came to the surface in his mind: The Wasteland.

The Fool didn't even want to set foot on it, but something told him that he had to go forward. There was no sign of The Lovers when he looked around, and the cloudy land had quite disappeared. All he could see in every direction was desolation, destruction, and stagnation. A most terrible sadness came over him. He felt that he could not even put a single foot forward, because there was no point, no reason to do so. He almost began to feel as though he was beginning to dry up, like the land itself. He felt so hopeless that he didn't even notice movement off to one side.

The next moment he felt himself picked up and thrown down onto the floor of a Chariot that was moving almost too fast to be possible. Yet, there was no driver, no horses, no engine. The Chariot seemed to move of its own accord.

At first The Fool was fearful, then he realised that The Chariot was carrying him away from the terrible Wasteland, and as he left it behind, so he began to feel better. Which was just as well, because in a few moments The Chariot came to a halt, and The Fool tumbled out, only to feel himself grabbed by invisible hands and pushed into a small, bare room. He heard the door close behind him with a clang and looked around and saw that he was in a place with hard, stony walls. There was only one tiny window, protected by bars of metal that made it quite impossible to escape. The door by which he had been admitted was closed fast and would not even move when he tried it (Prisoner).

A terrible sense of loss came over The Fool. He sat down on the floor, since there was nothing else to sit on, and hid his face in his hands. Tears fell between his fingers and made little circles on the dusty floor. All the sorrow he had felt while he was in The Wasteland came back to him, and now he thought he was in a place from which he could not escape. Was this the end of his journey?

(v)

The Fool had no idea how long he was in the prison. It might have been hours, or days, or weeks. The surprising thing was that he didn't feel thirsty or hungry in all that time—so maybe it was just a few moments, perhaps no more than an hour? Then suddenly the door to his cell opened, and two people who looked like soldiers came in and marched him outside. They were not particularly unfriendly, or harsh, but The Fool's spirits were so low by this time that he didn't really care.

The soldiers took The Fool across a wide courtyard, until they came to a place where a dais was set up. On it was set up a huge pair of scales, big enough to hold a person. Somewhere at the back of his mind, a thought came to him that he had been here before, that he had been weighed before. But why? At that moment, a very beautiful lady appeared, and even though he couldn't remember exactly where he'd seen her before, The Fool knew that she was a goddess, and that her name was Justice.

The soldiers indicated that The Fool should stand there and do nothing. He was quite happy to do that, because just to do nothing in the fresh air felt better than doing nothing in his tiny cell.

"So you are The Prisoner," said Justice. "I think we may have met before. Why do you think you are here?"

"I don't know," said The Fool miserably. "I was just looking at Wonder, then at some Lovers, then I was in a terrible place where I couldn't move at all, then I was put in the cell, and now I'm here." He looked up at the goddess, who seemed kindly as well as stern.

"I think I'm supposed to get onto the scales?" said The Fool.

"Quite right," answered the goddess. "In you get."

So The Fool climbed up into one of the bowls on the scale and sat down in the middle.

The scales didn't move at all.

"Ah," said Justice. "This is most unusual. It seems that you have no weight. That you are undecided, unable to choose what you want to do with your life. Would you say that is true?"

The Fool thought for a moment, then he nodded. "I think so," he said. "I know I had something to do, but I seem to have forgotten it."

"Very well then," said Justice. "I think you need to have some time to just think about it."

The Fool said nothing, thinking that he was going to be put back in the cell. But the Goddess waved a hand in his direction, and the next moment he found himself flying through the air, until his feet became entangled in the branches of a tree, and he ended up hanging upside down, with his head toward the ground (Hanged Man).

At first The Fool was rather worried, because he thought that all the blood would rush to his head and maybe come dashing out of his ears. But that didn't happen. Strangely, he began to feel a kind of euphoria, as though looking at everything from upside down made it feel different. He thought, "When I get free—if I get free—I know what I'm going to do next. I'm going to take some time to think and be alone and live on my own and talk to nobody."

As he thought this, the branches in which his feet were entangled suddenly released him, so that he fell to the ground and got up at once, unhurt. Something even stranger happened now, because as he stood there, The Fool felt wings sprouting from his back, and the next moment he was flying in the air. A wonderful sense of lightness filled him, and he found himself shouting out loudly, "I'm free!" (The Escape).

(vi)

The Fool flew on for a while, enjoying the sensation of being in charge of himself and deciding where he would go. The land below was an unrolled carpet of different kinds: lush, arid, tree-lined, and home to fields of golden wheat. Then The Fool saw some rocky outcrops, and in them was a small opening.

Down flew The Fool and landed on the ground. He went into the gap between the rocks and found himself in a small, dry cave. It must have had someone staying in it recently, although there was no one there at the moment, because he found the remains of a fire and signs of things being cooked. It was dark in there, especially as the sun started to go down, but The Fool remembered that in his pack was a lantern, and when he opened it he found it was already lit and sending its golden rays into the darkness.

The Fool felt his spirits rising. "I am The Hermit," he said, out loud. And somehow he remembered another occasion when he had spoken with someone who also called himself a hermit, and who spent all his time thinking and meditating and finding a way to understand the world. *That's what I'm going to do*, thought The Fool, and stirred the fire and sat down by it and, by the light of the lantern, began to think about all the things that had happened to him on his journey. And though at first he felt he didn't understand anything, gradually things began to make sense.

After a while, The Fool felt his eyes grow heavy, and he lay down and fell into a deep sleep. And in the sleep he began to dream. He dreamed that Sleep itself was more important than anyone realised. Not only did it bring rest after exertion, but it also brought Dreams. And as he dreamed about dreaming, The Fool realised that dreams held all kinds of answers, other ways of seeing and feeling, and that things that made no sense when awake were suddenly clear. In his sleep The Fool felt peaceful and quiet. For the first time since this journey began, he felt that he was really listening, not just to the things other people told him, but to his own thoughts.

(vii)

In the dream, The Fool saw himself standing on the prow of a boat and casting a great net over the side into the sea and pulling up huge catches of fish (Fisherman). At the same time, he knew they weren't just fish but opportunities, ideas, things worth doing, whether one knew the outcome or not. And as he looked at his shining catch, The Fool felt something he had not felt for a long time, and that was strength. And he remembered how one of the gifts he had been given long ago, on another journey, had been just that: Strength. And all the fears of his last few experiences—The Wasteland, The Prison, even Justice—seemed to fall away from him, and he remembered the promise he had made to The Empress and Emperor about teaching the secrets of Tradition, of the past, and of the things that could be learned. And though he didn't really think he knew very much yet, he knew that he had something to impart from his own journey.

Suddenly The Fool started laughing. *I am a Fool*, he said to himself. *Yet, I know how to guide people, how to show them which way to go. I do, I do! So I must be a Teacher.*

"Perhaps you are," said a voice, and The Fool woke from his revery/dream and saw a big man standing at the entrance to the cave. He wore rough clothing and carried a big shovel over his shoulder.

"I was just passing," he said. "I overheard your thoughts. Are you really a teacher?"

"I don't think so," said The Fool. "But I do have things to say."

"Well, you can say them to me if you like," said the big man. "I'm just on my way to work. You can come with me and tell me what you have to say as we go."

So The Fool and The Worker set off along the road together, and as they went, The Fool told his new companion about his journey, the people he had met, and the things he had learned. When he described The Wasteland, The Worker stopped for a moment and looked at him.

"That sounds like the kind of place that could do with my kind of work," he said. "I could dig the ground and divert some water from a stream to moisten it. That's the kind of work I like. If I help the land, the land helps me. What do you think?"

"That sounds like a great idea," said The Fool. "But I think it would need lots of people like you to do that."

"Well," said The Worker, "I have lots of friends. I'm going to tell them about this place, and we're going to go and see if we can turn it back into a good, fruitful piece of earth."

The Fool and The Worker walked on together for a while

in silence, each one thinking about The Wasteland and how it could be made better. After a while they came to the place where The Worker was busy. It was a little house, where the roof had fallen in, and The Worker was putting it back together, restoring it to the way it had been. The Fool stayed for a while and helped him, fetching and carrying slates. Around noon they shared a pleasant meal of bread and cheese and fresh water, and The Worker told The Fool about his other work, most of which employed digging. "You'd be surprised what I dig up sometimes," said The Worker. "It's a bit like life. The deeper you dig, the more you uncover. I once found some treasure that someone had buried. Would you like to see?"

"Yes, please," said The Fool, feeling excited at the thought of treasure. The Worker opened the rough bag that he carried and brought out the strangest thing. It looked like a Wheel carved out of old dark wood, and around the edge of the wheel were little seats, and in the seats sat tiny carved people. The Worker spun The Wheel a couple of times, and The Fool noticed how the people at the top became the people at the bottom and how the people at the bottom became the people at the top.

"Everything changes, you see," said The Worker. "Nothing stays the same."

The Fool looked at the little carving and, at the back of his mind, thought he'd seen something like it before, and that he'd been shown exactly the same thing that happened when The Wheel turned.

"I call it The Wheel of Fortune," said The Worker. "Things change so much, and you never know what's around the corner."

The Fool agreed, thinking about all the unexpected things

that had happened to him on his journey.

As the sun began to go down toward the horizon, The Fool took his leave of The Worker, who he really felt was a friend, and set off to go back to the cave, which felt to him like home.

(viii)

Before he'd gone very far, The Fool began to notice something disturbing. The ground under his feet no longer seemed firm and hard but trembled as though a huge hand was shaking the world, putting everything out of kilter. Suddenly The Fool began to feel afraid. He wasn't sure why, only that everything felt wrong (Chaos). He looked up at the sky and thought that everywhere he looked there were cracks, and he began to be afraid that the sky was going to fall on his head. He began to run along the road, thinking that once he got back to the cave, everything would be fine and he'd be safe. But under his feet, the ground began to give way, and bits of it began to fly up into the air, and dust rained down all over him, making him cough and making it hard to breathe.

Now The Fool was really afraid. He tried to run, but his feet didn't want to want to obey him. Then he fell down, and all around him the earth seemed to rise up as if it was going to cover him. But one of the gifts he had been given on that other journey was courage, and so he got up and kept running and stumbling on, until slowly the earth began to settle back down around him. Overhead, the cracks in the sky disappeared, and the sun came out. The Fool found that he could breathe again, and the air tasted sweet. Everything that had seemed chaotic and wrong settled down again.

Soon the welcoming shape of the cave mouth came into view, and The Fool hurried inside. He managed to get the fire started again and was soon warming his hands by the flames.

Soon after, he heard a sound outside and went to look. There he saw a man walking up and down, muttering to himself. He was dressed in a rather elegant suit, with a top hat. He seemed vaguely familiar to The Fool. When the man became aware of him, he stopped walking up and down and turned to look at The Fool. His face was very brown and wrinkled, but his eyes were bright.

"Oh," he said. "It's you."

"Yes," said The Fool, hesitantly.

"You don't remember me, do you?" said the man.

"I'm not sure," said The Fool.

"I'm Mr. Death," said the man. "Once upon a time I got you down from a tree."

"I'm sorry," said The Fool. "I don't really remember." Quietly, he was wondering if this was really Death, and if it might mean the end for him.

As if he had heard the thought, Mr. Death said, "I haven't come for you today. I just wanted to remind you how fragile you are, and how easily your life can change."

Then he sketched a shape in the air with his hands, which seemed like a window, and The Fool found himself looking through into another place, where a lot of people were walking around slowly in circles. Many of them were weeping, while others were shaking their fists in the air, as if they were angry with something that wasn't there. Others just walked along dumbly with their heads bowed, staring at the ground, or looking straight ahead of them and not seeing anything.

"These are The Sorrowful," said Mr. Death. "Every one of

them has lost something dear to them. Or taken a wrong turn. Or are just feeling sad for reasons they can't quite say. Most of them are afraid about what comes next."

"How can we help?" asked The Fool.

"Only they can help themselves," said Mr. Death. "A lot of them end up here." And he pointed through the window and The Fool saw a tall Tower with just one door and no windows. Quite a lot of The Sorrowful people went in through the door and soon appeared standing on the top of The Tower, looking out miserably at nothing.

As he looked, The Fool saw The Tower began to shake. Cracks spread all over it, and overhead the sky got very dark. Then there was a great flash of lightning. It struck The Tower, which began to fall. The Fool saw many of the people who had been standing at the top falling through the air, crying out as they fell. He immediately wanted to rush forward and help, but before he could do that, the window that Mr. Death had opened closed, and there was nothing to see.

"That's terrible," he said. "Those poor people."

"It's all just a dream," said Mr. Death. "But somewhere in the world it's happening right now. There's nothing I can do, except take the people away somewhere else."

The Fool shivered. "Do you mean the Land of the Dead?" he said.

Mr. Death nodded.

"What's it like there?" asked The Fool.

"That is a mystery," said Mr. Death. But it's not one you have to worry about just yet." As he finished speaking, suddenly he was not there anymore, having vanished without a trace.

The Fool went back into his cave and sat by the fire, thinking of all that he had seen. Then after a while, he began to get sleepy and curled up by the fire and fell asleep. And in his sleep, once again, The Fool began to dream. In this dream he was shown a story of some people who seemed really important, who believed that everything they did was for the best, and that no one could gainsay them. And at first they were very popular—everyone loved them and thought they were wonderful. Then things changed, and just like The Tower, fame and fortune crumbled away and they weren't popular anymore, and no one liked them (The Downfall).

Into The Fool's mind came thoughts of falling. He tried to remember more. He recalled The Worker's little Wheel— what did he call it?—The Wheel of Fortune. Just like the people who were at the top but then fell to the bottom. But who spun The Wheel? Or did it just turn of its own accord?

Another picture came to him—a strange being with horns and a tail who danced along the sky, smiling and laughing and urging everyone who saw him to join in the fun. But what *was* the fun? The Fool recalled something he had been told long ago, in another life or another journey—a being called by some The Devil, who was said to lure people to do what he wanted them to do. He made people angry as well, The Fool thought, or distressed; sometimes they became stuck like the ones he had just seen, or the ones on The Wheel who could not get off.

The Fool tried to think what might help these people, and at once he heard a voice say, "They should ask questions, of course!" Then he saw one of the people in the group begin to question everything: Why did this happen? What did this mean? Whose fault was it? Why were things the way they were? How were they supposed to be? But the more they questioned, the less certain they became. Until soon, they were so uncertain they couldn't decide what to do about anything. But still The Questioner, whose voice he had heard, continued to ask questions, and slowly things began to seem less difficult, less unfortunate, less complicated.

And in the dream, The Fool saw another group of people sitting and talking around a table. Among them were some who had been popular and fallen from grace; others were the ones who asked questions. The more time they spent together, the less complicated things became. At first, some of them seemed so broken and sorrowful that nothing that was said made any difference, but after a while the compassion of the others began to have an effect, and The Sorrowful ones began to recover. At first it was just a tiny amount, but gradually they became more and more comfortable with each other.

Once again the dream changed, and The Fool saw two people sitting opposite each other in a room. Both of them were talking, but neither seemed to be listening. One of the people kept on saying that they couldn't remember what had happened to them or why. How did we get to this place? Whose fault was it? (Forgetting). But the other person kept looking around and saying, "I remember everything that ever happened to me. I remember the choices I made—both good and bad. And I remember the things that inspired me" (Remembering).

After a while, the two people started to talk to each other, one reminding the other about what they had forgotten and remembered. As they talked, they became more and more bright and light and Merry. The last thing The Fool saw of them, they were laughing and joking with each other.

The Fool awoke with a start, and when he opened his eyes he saw that he was no longer alone in his cave, but that a very beautiful lady was sitting with him. In each hand she held a small cup, and she was pouring water from one to the other. And each time she did that, the water changed colour, from blue to red to green and so on. An absolute rainbow of shades.

The Fool watched in fascination, until he found that the Lady was looking at him (Temperance).

"So you're still looking?" she said, as if she knew him.

The Fool nodded. "Yes," he said. "I am."

"And what have you found out so far?" asked the Lady.

"I found that working together can help," said The Fool. "And that those who think only of themselves fall from grace and have to start over again. And I found that those who let sorrow overwhelm them, even when the reason is good, feel worse and can't find their way home. And some of them forget and others remember . . ."

"Goodness, that's a lot of new things you've found out," said the Lady. "I remember you were once interested only in finding out who you were meant to be."

"I'd still like to know that," said The Fool. "But somehow it doesn't seem so important at the moment."

"You may actually be becoming wise," said the Lady. She stopped pouring the water from cup to cup for a moment. It was blue as it settled down. She offered The Fool a drink, and he accepted it gladly, realising he felt very thirsty from all the dust and destruction in the air just recently. The water tasted very blue somehow, and it quenched his thirst better than anything he had ever known.

The Lady went back to pouring the water from cup to cup, and as The Fool watched her, he began to feel sleep coming over him.

"I think I feel another dream coming on," he said. But the

Lady was no longer there. The cave seemed suddenly very sad and lonely to The Fool. "I'm not sure I like being on this journey so much," he muttered. "What's the point anyway. It feels like I'm just going in circles."

He sat grumpily on the floor and watched as the flames died in his little fire. He didn't even feel like lighting it again, then he realised it was a long time since he had eaten—sharing The Worker's lunch seemed no more than a memory.

"I used to think I knew nothing," The Fool said out loud, though there was no one to hear. "Now I think I know too much."

(ix)

Cold, alone, hungry, and sad, The Fool settled down and fell asleep. But this time his dream was different.

He saw himself marching along the road. Many people followed him, and they were all listening to every word he said. The Fool felt very important and thought of lots of things to say. Not all of them were true, but that didn't matter. All that mattered was how important he felt.

Then he saw someone come forward from the crowd. This person carried a silver dish full of water, and when he locked into it he saw things that others—including The Fool—could not.

The Fool suddenly felt very foolish. What on earth was he doing pretending to be so wise, when this simple person with a dish of water could see everything so clearly? Then The Fool noticed that The Diviner never once said what the visions meant, but left people to discover what there was to find.

That's a good idea, The Fool thought. *No one really knows enough to say what's true for others. They need to find Truth for themselves.*

With this, The Fool woke up, surprised to find himself no longer in his little cave, but outside. It was night, and above him the stars were shining. As The Fool looked up, marvelling at how many there were, one particular star began to wink at him, and he heard a voice addressing him.

"You seem to have found out a great deal," said the voice, which The Fool felt must be coming from the Star. "But have you learned how to be a Clown?"

"A Clown?" said The Fool. "That's what I thought I was already."

"Not so," said the voice of The Star. "A Clown is someone who makes people laugh—a Fool is someone people laugh at."

"Isn't that the same thing?" asked The Fool.

"No," said The Star. "It's completely different. Let The Moon explain it."

The Fool felt strangely light-headed suddenly, but when he turned around he saw the most beautiful lady, dressed in blue, who smiled and waved to him as though they were old friends.

"Can you help me tell the difference between a Fool and a Clown?" asked The Fool.

"I think," said The Moon, "that the difference is in how you feel. When someone sees *you*, they think you are someone who's bound on a great adventure, travelling in search of wisdom and answers to the things that people are always asking about. This doesn't make them laugh, even though some of the things you do and say might be considered laughable . . . with The Clown, it's all about making people laugh. And whatever happens, it's nearly always about things going wrong, about falling over without getting hurt, then jumping up and going on, and falling over again. People are strange the way they find these things funny, so sometimes I call him the False Fool, because he makes people laugh for strange reasons."

All of this made The Fool think very deeply about himself. *What kind of fool am I?* he murmured.

"A very kind and generous one," answered The Moon. "My brother, The Sun, also knows a lot about this. He's so full of joy, and light, of course, that he's almost bursting with fun. Do you see?"

As she spoke, everything got very bright indeed, so that The Fool had to shade his eyes, but when he looked around, The Moon was nowhere to be seen, and the sky was bright, and where the air had been cool before, now it was warm.

The Sun shone down on The Fool, who found that he was, inexplicably, happy. "You see," said a great booming voice from above him in the sky, "where there is light, there's laughter."

"I'm sorry I can't see you," said The Fool, shading his eyes. "You're just too bright."

"That happens quite a lot," said The Sun. "But I keep shining. I have to light up the world, you see, and make sure everything grows. Am I not right, Nature?"

The Fool heard a curious rustling noise behind him, and when he turned around he found himself looking at a most curious person. This person was green, every kind of green The Fool had ever seen. It seemed at the moment like a very wise tree, and two great greenish-brown eyes stared out at him from within a tangle of greenery.

"You've seen quite a lot of my work recently," said Nature, in its strange rustling voice. "You saw what can happen when I get forgotten or driven away. The earth becomes a Wasteland.

But you know, even somewhere as dry and barren as that can be made fresh again. Everything can be repaired, replaced, renewed, refreshed—if people want to." He sounded quite sad, The Fool thought.

"I am," answered Nature, as if it had heard the thought. "But I'm here for as long as people want me. For as long as people see me and understand me. I have great patience. I've been here, after all, much longer than you, and I'll probably be here a long time after you've gone."

"Does it have to be like that?" asked The Fool.

"Definitely not," said Nature. "But only you can decide how it will go. Not you personally," it added, "but all the people out there, so many of whom seem to me to be quite lost. I think they've forgotten who I am, and how important I am."

As he heard this, The Fool saw a picture in his mind. Hundreds of people wandering in a great hall with many doors, heads down, staring at the ground, muttering to themselves, seeming lost (The Lost). The picture was there only for a moment, but it made The Fool feel very sad.

"I wish there was something I could do," he said.

"But there is," said Nature. "All it takes is a few people like you to decide you don't want the future to be the way it is at the moment. There's plenty of opportunity for renewal, for restoration. It's up to you."

"I would say it's up to everyone," said a new voice. The Fool looked over his shoulder, and there was standing a figure he thought felt familiar, though he couldn't say where or when he'd seen her before.

"You see," said the lady, "it's all about using your Judgement."

"But don't I have to be really wise to do that?" said

The Fool.

"Of course," answered the lady. "But the more you try, the more you learn. Mostly you just have to listen."

At that moment, The Fool heard a chorus of voices. "We are listening!" they said, in overlapping tones. There behind him were a group of people, and the thing he noticed immediately about them was that they all had big round eyes, and large ears, and that they were focused in a way that almost no one he had ever met was focused. "We listen all the time," they said. "We pay attention. We hear the truth. It's all about harmony" (The Listeners).

As the voices said this, it seemed to The Fool that they were all singing, and that the sound was one of the most beautiful sounds he had ever heard.

"Is there anything in particular you listen for?" he asked.

"We listened to everything," said the chorus of voices. "But especially we listen to History."

"History?" said The Fool. "I thought that was all over and done with."

"Far from it!" said a new voice. At once The Fool was no longer standing under the vast night sky, but in a big room, shelved from floor to ceiling, every bit of space crammed with books, some old, some new. In the middle of the room was a lectern, and on it sat the biggest book The Fool had ever seen. It must have had thousands of pages.

The Fool stared in wonder at all the books and remembered how The Hierophant had been reading from a similar tome, in which he showed The Fool great truths. He found himself wishing he could live for hundreds of years and do nothing but read. A chuckle. The Fool realised it came from the vast book.

"It's good you feel that way," said the voice. "But if you did, you would never go outside and see the world. I am History," it went on. "I remember everything that ever happened—even the bits that have been lost."

"Someone else told me about remembering things," said The Fool, thinking of The Emperor and Empress. "I understand about Tradition, but is that the same as History?"

"It's all connected," said History, "but there's much more to it than that."

"Why do we need to remember these things?" said The Fool.

"Lots of reasons," said History. "The biggest is that it shows the mistakes that were made over the centuries. If we hadn't done certain things, other things wouldn't have happened. And if we had done some things, then again other things might *not* have happened. It never changes. History goes on; it rolls along like a river. And every now and then there's a rock, or a stone, that interrupts it or sends it off in another direction. We never know what's coming next. Even I don't know. But often, looking back, I can see the way things might happen. That's why History is so important. If you like, you could say we learn by our mistakes."

"I think I see what you mean," said The Fool. "I suppose it's really important to look at all of this." He looked around the room full of books. "But who can possibly remember everything that happened?"

"Ah," said the voice of History. "That's my job. All you have to do is listen and watch."

"Watching is very important," said another voice. The Fool looked around. At first he couldn't see anywhere the voice might have come from. Then he looked up and saw something that looked like a bubble floating near the ceiling of the room. Inside he could just see a blurry face, which looked down at him. He couldn't tell who or even what kind of a face it was—kind or cross, peaceful, or mad.

"Who are you?" asked The Fool.

"I am The Observer," said the voice from inside the bubble. "I watch everything that happens. When someone has a thought, I see it. I try to see where it will go, what it will lead to. I try to see the whole picture. You could say I'm vigilant."

"But why do you do that?" asked The Fool.

"Because of the patterns," answered the voice. "There are patterns everywhere. Patterns in the way people think. Patterns in what they do. Patterns. Patterns. Patterns. I watch for those, and when I see one I try to make the person thinking the thought be aware of them. That way they get a clearer idea of what the thought was about, and where it may lead, and even where it came from."

"I wish I knew what my patterns were," said The Fool.

"Would you like me to show you?" said the voice of The Observer.

"Yes, please," said The Fool.

"From where I am, it looks something like this," said the voice. And as it spoke, the room began to dissolve around him. The last thing to go was the big book of History.

(x)

The Fool finds himself standing at the edge of an immeasurable Ocean. Great waves come rolling in and crash on the shore just ahead of him, causing him to back away in alarm. Far out in the distance, he sees what he thinks are ships being tossed about on the water, and among them a huge fishtail that rises from the deep to slap the water.

The Fool steps back even farther and looks along the shore in either direction just to see where he might go. He has to admit that The Ocean made him feel uncomfortable. It was too big, and too fierce, and too lonely. He cannot imagine going out upon it, being caught up and pushed from one place to another by the waves, having no control over anything. And what if he went overboard? What then? The Fool doesn't like the idea of drowning one bit, so he turns his back on The Ocean and looks at where he came from instead.

At first he can't see anything familiar. The road leads into the distance and passes over fields, and across rivers and through forests and over hills, and in the distance there are mountains.

Where shall I go now? wonders The Fool. *This has been such a long journey. Will there ever be an end?*

As he thinks this, he notices a particular Road, running from the sea inland. Of all the roads he has been on, this one is the widest, the smoothest, and somehow the most definite.

I think this is my direction, murmurs The Fool. And he sets off along it with fresh determination.

He hasn't gone far when he comes to a place where the road divided into three. Right in the middle was a signpost, with three arms pointing in different directions. The one pointing to the left says WISDOM. The one in the middle says FEAR. The one on the right says PAST AND FUTURE.

Which way to go?

At that moment, The Fool sees someone walking toward him on the path that says it leads to Wisdom. A tall and beautiful woman, who had the most peaceful, clever, kindly, knowledgeable, ageless look of anyone he could remember seeing—even the Goddess of Justice, or Temperance, or the Priestess, or Judgement, or The Moon—though when he thinks about it, The Fool thinks that this lady looks a little bit like all of them.

"Excuse me," asks The Fool. "Are you Wisdom?"

The Lady nods.

"Have you come here to teach me?" The Fool asks.

"I will teach anyone who is willing to listen," says Wisdom.

"Well," says The Fool, "can you tell me which of these roads I should take?"

"In time," says Wisdom, "you should take them all. You've already felt Fear in the Past, but you need to feel it again in the Future."

"But why?" asks The Fool.

"Because Fear teaches you to take care," says Wisdom. Then she smiles. "And of course it also stops you in your tracks, stops you making decisions, wrong or right. That's another good reason for understanding what it is to be afraid. Because only then can you overcome it."

"I think I understand," says The Fool. He looks again at the signpost. "So if that road leads to you, Wisdom, and that road leads to Fear, where does the third road lead to?"

"That should be clear enough," says Wisdom. "It says Past and Future."

"But why do I need to go to the past?" asks The Fool. "And even if I can, why would I want to go to the future?"

"Because both of them show possibilities. The Past shows you the things that were and how they lead to things that are. The Future is being written all the time, but sometimes we get a glimpse of it. And sometimes that glimpse refers to something in The Past. In one of those places you may find answers. But remember that now you are in the present. Haven't you been looking for these things all this time?"

The Fool nods.

"It's true, I have," he says. "And I think I've begun to see some of them. But it's such a lot to keep in my head."

"Then let your thoughts go," says Wisdom. "Let them be free. Let them run about and enjoy themselves. For that way lies Healing."

As she says this, The Fool feels a very strange sensation. It's as if a hand reached out and touched him on the shoulder, though when he looks, no one is there. It certainly wasn't Wisdom. But whoever it is, or whatever it is, or wherever it is, he suddenly feels as though every difficult, harsh, angry, bitter, uncertain thing he has ever felt melts away. He feels as though a moment ago, he had been very old, older than anyone he'd ever met. But in that moment he became young again. He thinks for a moment about the time when he began this journey—such a long time ago, it seems. *Perhaps that's what history meant?*

"Perhaps it is," says the voice of Wisdom—but The Fool cannot see her any longer. Nor can he see the road. Or the signpost. Or the sky. Instead, he finds that part of himself has moved along, way out into the depths of space. From there he can see The World—the whole wide World. He sees it turning gently, and the continents sliding past. And he sees lights shining out from it—little patches of light he thinks might be cities, or maybe just places where people live who think thoughts that are light and bring light with them.

The Fool thinks of all the wonderful things he has seen. All the extraordinary people he has met. He remembers every one of them, and every word they said to him, and every thought he has had as a result. He even remembers another journey, an old journey, on which he learned so much. But now he thinks, *I'm on a new journey, and it's still not over. Because journeys don't have to have endings, journeys can go on and on—and as long as you're ready to enjoy them, and prepared for anything that may happen, every journey is exciting, and wonderful.*

And as he thinks this, there comes to him a single word. A word that seems to sum up all the possibilities that he or anyone has ever had—all the choices, all the wrong turnings, all the right paths, all the ideas and beliefs and truths and lies and wonder and terror, the vastness of the ocean, the wonder of the heavens, the music of everything.

All of these things are summed up in one word: *Eternity*. And as that word rings in his head, The Fool comes Full Circle in his journey—back to the beginning, which is also the end.

And in the distance he thinks he hears a small dog, barking.

FIN

PART

THREE

WORKING WITH
THE FOOL'S NEW JOURNEY TAROT

READINGS AND SPREADS

Fool's Dream

Aiming his smile
at the sky like an arrow
Fool slipped on the green
lay beneath his shadow,

Fool met Death.
Didn't know her.
Tried a joke.
Death laughed.
Live another day Fool
She said.

READING THE JOURNEY

Most traditional Tarot readings concern themselves with the relationship of the cards to each other and their placing in a spread. While some of our suggested methods include this style of reading, for the most part we see the cards as telling a story. Just as in the two fables included here, the sequence itself drives the path of The Fool, so the methodology we are working with is that the cards represent the client's personal journey in the same way, and that they should be read as a sequence that tells a story.

TAKING SOUNDINGS

Once you have familiarised yourself with the sequence of the cards and their intrinsic meanings, you are ready to begin playing with them. This will often entail creating your own story, shown by the cards, in which you will find the answer you seek. Be relaxed in your first attempts, as you will find that the new cards and their meanings will throw up many questions. This is in line with what we believe to be the essential purpose of Tarot—not so much to answer our questions, but to encourage us to ask *ourselves* for answers. Most professional readers will tell you that the cards really are just pieces of card with images on them—it's the relationship between us as reader and the deeply powerful Tarot imagery that creates the divinatory magic and the questions we ask of them.

However, since most Tarot readings are based on asking for answers, we need to consider how and what we ask—how we frame our question in order to get the best possible answer. We need to think about this carefully. The simpler the question, the more direct the answer you will receive. Avoid yes/no, either/or questions, as these tend to muddy the waters and give you indecisive answers. Ones beginning with "Should I . . ." mean you have abandoned responsibility for your actions and handed them over to the Tarot. Thus, instead of asking, for example, "Should I move in with Dave," it would be better to ask, "What qualities does Dave have that would make him the right partner for me?," and so on. Some good formats are the following:

> What is the likely consequence of . . .?
> Please show me how I might . . .
> Please guide me . . .
> Help me to see the issue clearly . . .
> Show me how to move forward . . .

These are important considerations for any reader, whether seeking answers for ourselves or for others. To begin with, you may find it easier to ask simple, direct questions, using just two or three cards that do not require a lengthy commentary. Here are a couple of basic examples. (In these trial runs, we asked the client to respond later with any outcome from the reading. Normally we do not get to hear what occurs.)

Two-Card Reading

14 THE CHARIOT   16 THE PRISONER

Jo was an experienced writer whose work was beginning to attract attention, so that she was considering employing a publicist to raise her profile. She wondered what she should do next and what effect it would be likely to have on promoting her work. She did a simple two-card reading for this and drew two cards:

The Chariot seemed to suggest that moving forward, the prospects were good, since everything about this card spoke of movement and drive. She gave particular attention to the words from the description:

The heart as well as the head must rule if one is to obtain one's desires, and mastery over the worldly life and the ability to transcend everyday concerns is central to its understanding. The twin horses of emotion and intellect, disharmony and calm, require balance, enabling progress to be undertaken with fewer of the stresses and strains of everyday life. Consider how hard you work to build your career, winning fame and creating influence around you. Mastery of skill or ability brings a successful outcome; self-confidence and self-discipline enable the harnessing of abilities.

The second card, The Prisoner, suggested that Jo could find herself trapped into a cycle of needing to provide more material for her potential publicist to work on. She particularly noted,

As we progress on our own journeys we will, unless we are supremely lucky, find ourselves taking a wrong turn, being forced into a situation where we cannot move either forward or back.

Uncertain how she felt about this, she elected to choose a third card:

This was The Wheel of Fortune, which speaks of rising to greater heights, but also the possibility of falling from them. She took this to indicate that working with a high-powered publicist would demand too much of her at this point in her career. She decided to postpone the decision until she had sold more of her work. Shortly after this, she was taken up by a commercial publisher, larger than any she had worked with before, and found her name speaking for itself.

Three-Card Reading

For this reading, the client, David, a talented musician, wanted to know what the consequences might be for getting back together with an old girlfriend. His three-card reading was as follows:

The first card, Beauty, seemed particularly appropriate and meaningful to him. The girl in question was a great beauty, and one of the reasons for their breakup was his jealousy regarding other men who had noticed her striking looks when they were out together.

The second card, The Hermit, he recognised as representing himself. Though reasonably outgoing, he still longed for quiet times even when he and his girlfriend were party going—something she enjoyed far more than he. He also read that

The Hermit contemplates the passage of events in order to find a true meaning, but also acknowledges the passage of time and the way this impacts upon the issues under consideration. Such acknowledgment allows the seeker to be detached, enabling a clearer view of the circumstances that have brought the problem into being.

This made him think that he needed to consider his next actions carefully. His ex had indicated that she might be willing to get back together; he need to be sure that this would bring happiness to them both, not just to one or the other.

Turning to the third card, The Worker, which seemed to him to be the decider in the issue, he read that

> *The Worker knows his or her craft and applies their skills to whatever work is required. . . . They offer a service freely and, it is hoped, with joy. In a reading the card represents every one of us, and as such it is influential in any enquiry or issue raised. Any kind of work is covered by this, and though we have portrayed a very basic figure of the worker, sitting behind a desk or digging a hole in the earth are equally relevant in any reading where this card appears.*

For him the work was his music, and the description relating to the card chimed with his feelings about what he did. But how did this extend to his relationship? The more he puzzled over this, the more he realised that his work was, in the end, more important than his feelings for his ex. In the week following this reading, David gave a recital of music and saw the ex in the audience. Love blossomed again in his heart, and the two became a couple again following this event.

Five-Card Reading

This client was concerned that he had not received a payment already overdue. Was the company reneging? Were they in trouble? He was extremely angry and distressed by this, having sent reminders that had been ignored. He asked the Tarot what the cause was in a straight four-card spread, with a fifth card to anchor the response.

The question was phrased as "What is holding back payment?"

The four cards were

3: The Shadow. 47: Judgement. 28: Death. 6: Tradition.

The fifth card was

44: The Star

Looking at these, the first indication, The Shadow, clearly pointed to the feeling of desperation experienced by the reader, produced by a feeling that the company was not being honest but was concealing something. He was looking at the shadowy side and was mainly concerned with his own possible loss rather than others who might be affected. The second card, Judgement, clearly called out for the need for fair dealing for the client, but also that he needed to weigh all the possibilities and be prepared to face the loss rather than struggling against it. He should refrain from being judgemental until he had all the facts. He might also need to remain flexible whichever way the scales were weighted. The third card, Death, showed that things had ground to a halt, with no response from the company. It suggested that the outcome was inevitable and that a negative outcome was possible. The fourth card, Tradition, spoke of the need for traditional justice and values, and that the situation was part of a need on the part of the client to learn from the circumstances rather than becoming lost in dispute. A Traditional approach, including writing a letter rather than emailing, was also suggested. The final, closing card, The Star, was all about harmony, self-possession, and confidence—all of which were required in this situation.

The overall reading suggested that the client had reacted badly to the delays and possibly made his situation worse by his complaints and feelings of anger toward the company. If, instead, he chose to be calm and self-possessed, seeking a more balanced view and allowing an honest judgement to take place, he would feel better. It also warned that the outcome was by no means certain to be favourable.

With this on board, the client became calmer and elected to wait a further week. During this time, he received an apology from the company. An error in accounting had caused the glitch. The payment came through within another few days.

Fate or Destiny?

Considering the examples given here, we need to remember that a Tarot spread is not a self-fulfilling prophecy. Many Tarot commentators, readers and writers alike, have suggested it is best to see any Tarot spread as merely a sighting of the possibilities available, or as a photograph of a single moment. This way you will not attempt to live up to what the reading has told you, but more simply to use it for life navigation, as you would treat the general coordinates of a map as general guidance. The landscape on a map is fixed, but when travelling through it, you deal with weather and other conditions that cause you to accelerate, stop, or seek alternative routes.

Above all, when working with any divinatory tool, it is important to understand the differences among fate, destiny, and free will, because two of these terms are used very loosely and sometimes interchangeably by practitioners of the art.

Fate is woven from our unique appearance in the apparent world: we are born at a time and place of two parents, whose physical characteristics, ancestral tendencies, and gifts you inherit from them. We can do little to change these things, apart from some superficial aspects such as dyeing one's hair a different colour. But if we are born blind, then we are unlikely to be able to see, except with our other senses. We have to learn to work with the fate we were born with.

Destiny is the path you forge in life, drawing upon the innate gifts and potential that you have. Being naturally talented with artistic skills will not make you an artist unless you train, practice, and become recognized by others as one. Resting on the laurels of your destiny is a mistake. If someone divines that you are destined to do something, then you will almost certainly not achieve it without your free will and engagement. Accidental destiny (sometimes called serendipity) may be portrayed in films or books, but even there, free will must enter into things.

Free will is the ability to be passive or active in our lives. Living passively, we achieve little. Living with engagement makes our lives active. Free will determines whether we say yes or no to opportunity. Responding in the negative is as important as responding in the affirmative. When is an opportunity a temptation or a false trail and distraction? It is usually when you turn away from your natural inclination and common sense.

Interpreting the Cards

When you first begin to read the cards for yourself, you call upon a vast array of resources, which include focusing upon

1. the primary visual impact of the image on the card;

2. the written and suggested meanings for each individual card;

3. the card's position in a spread;

4. the juxtaposition/association of one card with another;

5. what story, impression, or tendency is emerging from the whole spread; and

6. the relevance of the spread to the issue or question that triggered it.

If you are a beginner to Tarot, this will be quite enough to occupy your attention. Remember that there is no "right" way to read and interpret a reading. The more you work with the cards, the more you will understand what a large part intuition plays in helping you to interpret.

The possible combinations of 60 cards, as in this new deck in their upright and reversed positions, are vast, and there is little point trying to remember or prepare for any particular combination. However, we suggest pairing the cards daily, drawing two random cards and practicing making a story come alive from them and revealing what meaning might lie hidden within.

Your imagination will suggest ideas, stories, and themes automatically, because you are already wired with circuits of understanding. As you become more proficient at interpreting the cards, you will find that listening to the promptings therein, entertaining the possibilities that they suggest, and exploring them in greater depth will take you ever more deeply into *The Fool's New Journey*.

Reality has many alternative channels, and the cards will often show these to you. Sometimes a small detail will speak louder than the main substance of the image. For example, what path dictates The Fool's choice in The Road? There is more to deciding what way to go than may seem obvious. Divination is a skill that is largely oral and hands on rather than just about the text, so practice divining in a way that works for you.

Dealing with Reversals

We have provided reversed meanings throughout *The Fool's New Journey Tarot*, so that when a reversed card shows up in a spread, as it is often likely to do, no matter how many times you "straighten up" the deck, it is worth noting it, even if you've decided to ignore reversals because you are an apprentice or don't use them normally. A reversal may signify a blockage, some self-sabotage, or a factor that you've not taken into account. Again, if you find a card difficult to read in any position or you feel ambivalent about it, try consulting the reversed meanings for a change. Some cards read better reversed than upright. By doing this you are not fudging the issue, but shaping your own approach both to the question and the response of the cards.

Throughout this Tarot, there are many opportunities to engage with reversals as well as with all the cards' upright meanings. With the 60 triumphs of *The Fool's New Journey Tarot*, you can explore hidden aspects of the reading by looking at opportunities you might be missing, directional changes you may be resisting, and what possible blockages need to be cleared. In time, you should learn to assess things from your own perspectives, your relationship with others, and the impact of your life upon the wider world.

Enhancing and Rectifying Cards

When a card seems unreadable, no matter how many times you consider it, it often helps to draw another card to enhance it, so that you begin to perceive its resonance more clearly. Lay the new card beside the unreadable card: Does it stand in front of or behind it? Try the different positions and see for yourself, noting the interplay between the two cards, and so draw out the themes that your intuition is revealing. This process is called "enhancing" the card. Now look at the rest of the spread and see if the enhancement has demystified that area of the reading.

You may decide you need to "rectify" it, especially if one card makes you unhappy or you feel hemmed in by the prospect it offers you. This is not something that you need to avoid. Changing a card is merely another way of asking the Tarot to give a more nuanced answer. In the process of rectification, you consult with the pack to help you see what other possibilities or resources you had failed to notice. When you meet difficulties, you can

- draw the next card to give you some advice about it—does it suggest an opportunity, a change of direction, or a blockage that is holding you up? What encouragement are you offered?

- draw the next card as a companion to help you through this into other possibilities. How does it support you?

- draw another card as a practical way of seeing what action to take next. What intuitive action comes to you when you look at the card?

- overlap the original card with the new card that rectifies it in your reading and consider the possibilities it offers the whole spread.

Reading for Yourself and Others

Many diviners have noticed that reading for yourself is less easy than reading for others, but it is just as easy if you keep certain things in mind. When you read for yourself, take notes in which you outline the direction your reading takes you. Draw diagrams even, using your own formulae, drawings, and symbols. By recording findings in this way, you can check back and forward to see what changes are already happening or what is still stuck.

As soon as you cross the border into reading for others, you encounter someone else's needs, hopes, and expectations, as well as their assumptions about what divination is about. These cards reveal a snapshot of the current situation, suggesting ways through and over problems rather than pronouncing fixed coordinates. As the client makes decisions, so changes will begin to happen.

- Ensure that the location is suitable for undisturbed readings.

- Encourage the client to frame the question skillfully (see above, "Taking Soundings").

- Let the reading unfold like a story rather than a prediction. For example, "The way ahead offers these possibilities," rather than "You will go here or there."

- If none of the spreads in this book are appropriate, list all the client's questions about an issue and make these the positions of a customized spread.

- If you don't understand a card, move on to the next, returning to it later. Invite the client to choose unseen one or more cards from the deck to enhance or amplify the reading. Read the troublesome card in relation to the rest of the cards drawn.

- Reinforce strong or warning messages with commonsense and practical advice. Avoid negative predictions and always respect the client's opinions. Read the cards in ways that empower your clients rather than create despondency, or dependency, on you or the cards.

- Conclude by asking the client to formulate what s/he understands from the reading, or what actions they intend to take, modify, or change.

The marks of a good diviner are discretion, compassion, and nonjudgemental neutrality. We hear the voice of Tarot best when we create questions and divination requests from the point of need.

With all of this in mind, here are some spreads especially designed for use with *The Fool's New Journey Tarot*. Note that, as mentioned above, if you are accustomed to appointing specific meanings to the positions in the spread (e.g., past, present, future; positive or negative; allies and challengers), we have chosen not to do this. All the spreads here are intended to be read in a connected sequence, forming an account of the client's individual journey as the whole of the deck outlines that of The Fool. For those who prefer working in this way, we have included some suggested meanings for each position.

THE FOOL'S OWN SPREAD

(Six Cards)

This spread is, like all the journeys undertaken by The Fool—and those of us who follow in his footsteps—seemingly aimless and wandering. But within it, thanks to the innate wisdom of the Tarot, we find meanings that may seem unrelated but that are actually clear signposts for our engagement with life.

Our sample reading here was made for a man of middle age who felt he had taken a wrong turn in his life and wondered how he might get back on track. This seemed the perfect spread.

These were the cards we drew:

1: The Emperor
2: The Sun
3: The Lovers
4: Strength
5: Justice
6: Escape

1: WHERE

2: I

3: AM

4: GOING

6: DAY

5: THIS

Interestingly, we noticed that five out of the six cards drawn were from the older classical Tarot. This suggested that our client could be rooted more in the past than the present—but we looked ahead through the reading to see where it would lead.

The Emperor represented the motivation of the client himself—who possessed the inner certainty and drive that had led him to be highly regarded in his profession. *The Sun*, representing the light by which he lived, amplified this, suggesting that his path, though he felt uncertain of it, was actually right for him. *The Lovers*, the root of his being or existence, we felt had more to do with his own view of himself—and that he was actually more happy about his life and direction than appeared from his question. *Strength*, his sense of identity and direction, told us that he had the energy and determination to go in whichever direction he chose—whether to stay with his current path or move to another. *Justice* indicated that he was an honourable and farsighted person (he laughed aloud at this card and eventually told us that he was a successful barrister!). The final card, *Escape*, which could refer to a holiday or break, also suggested to us that our client had a strong desire to change his life course—despite the very evident indication of the whole reading to the contrary. We discussed this in some detail, and in the end the client said that he needed to consider the whole matter some more. In fact, he told us that the request for a reading had come from a light-hearted impulse, but that the cards implied that he was truly dissatisfied. We suggested that he pull a final card to see if this changed or agreed with the summary we had given. He agreed and drew *Hope*. We read him the final paragraph of the card's meaning:

In a reading, Hope can turn aside the darkness and show the way to discover healing and joy in the face of adversity. She brings a positive breath of fresh air to any situation and supports us in our search for answers and help. Above all, Hope offers us balance and truth and opens the way forward. She is one of the best-aspected cards in the deck and should always be recognised as having a powerful influence upon the whole reading.

Our client considered this carefully and finally agreed that the accuracy of the reading was such that it clearly told him that his moment of doubt was a temporary glitch. He decided he would take a holiday with his family before returning to work. He later contacted us from a rented house overlooking the sea and told us that he felt the cards had been right. The Fool's wandering circuit had shown him a true record of his life to date.

As a further extension of this, here are some suggested meanings for each position, on the basis of the words that accompany each place.

Where = motivation
I = identity/self
Am = being/existence
Going = direction
This = action
Day = now

THE WEIGHING-THE-ODDS SPREAD

(Eight Cards)

Even The Fool must have serious moments. When we find ourselves needing guidance for more-heavyweight issues, this is the spread for us. It is read in two lines, the uppermost, read from left to right, representing the pros of the current situation, and the lower, read from right to left, presenting the cons. By combining these, we find that the underlying pattern or cause of the issue is clearly revealed.

1: The Devil   2: Tradition   3: Hope   4: Strength

5: The Hierophant   6: The Magician   7: The Merry   8: The Listeners

We utilized this spread when a client asked us what the consequences might be of his selling his current home and moving to the other side of the world. Clearly this was a serious question, and we felt it demanded a serious response. As had been discovered in previous readings, the top line best represented the positive while the lower line indicated negative aspects. We also asked him to cut and shuffle the cards and to draw eight cards for himself

Here are the cards our client drew:

1: The Devil
2: Tradition
3: Hope
4: Strength
5: The Hierophant
6: The Magician
7: The Merry
8: The Listeners

Reading from left to right along the top line, as if unfurling a story, we began with *The Devil*. This inevitably suggested an element of uncertainty, even mockers, of our client's intention. The second card, *Tradition*, indicated that he was deeply rooted in his current life and home. *Hope* put, as ever, a positive spin on the situation, confirming that the client really believed in the impulse to move to a distant country and start afresh. *Strength* told us that he had the energy and will to carry out his intention.

This completed the top line, which were the pros of the situation. We then read the second line, as cons, in reverse order from right to left. The sixth card was *The Hierophant*, which told us of the presence, whether within our client him-self or embodied by a friend, to open the way and make the move happen. *The Magician*, which followed, turned the idea back upon itself, implying that our client was either fooling himself or being manipulated by an unscrupulous person. *The Merry* followed and in this context suggested that there was a degree of falsely positive feeling about the intended move. The final card, *The Listeners*, said to us that the client needed to reconsider his position and to listen to the advice of friends as well as his own intention.

While he agreed in principle with this, our client was open to a final confirmational reading through the upper and low-er lines to see how they worked in pairs rather than as oppos-ing strategies. This gave us *The Devil* and *The Hierophant*, as a first pair, which, read together, again implied a mischievous person (or inner intent) within the question. The second set, *Tradition* and *The Magician*, seemed to empower this, consid-ering *The Magician's* traditional perspective as a trickster. The next set, *Hope* and *The Merry*, both indicated a more positive outcome, as did the last pair, *Strength* and *The Listeners*. The emphasis on these told our client that he should pay attention to other views and bring the strength he possessed to bear upon the issue. We heard later that a number of friends and family members had presented him with some good reasons not to make up his mind too quickly.

(Nine Cards)

Our journeys may take us anywhere—inward, outward, upward, or down. The mystery of Tarot is that whichever way we choose, it knows what to tell us. This spread takes the form of a spiral. Again, this is intended to be read as an ongoing story, featuring the client's own journey.

For this reading, the client, Stephanie, was trying to decide between two colleges, at both of which she had been offered a place. One was prestigious, offering an immediate benefit to potential career opportunities, but was also expensive; the other was less well known, though equally professional, but was much cheaper. Though she knew that the cards could not choose for her, she needed some help to clarify her own issues and concerns fuelling her feelings of uncertainty. She drew the following nine cards:

1: Strength
2: The Questioner
3: The Lovers
4: The Devil
5: Justice
6: The Road
7: The Moon
8: The Teacher
9: Tradition

1

2

3

4

9

5

8

6

7

We began our reading at the outside of the spiral, moving toward the centre and the possible outcome (it would be equally appropriate to begin at the centre and work outward). *Strength*, as always in a reading, fuelled the client's desire to find the best place for her to continue her studies. *The Questioner*, the second card, perfectly expressed her own inner questioning and indecision. The third card, *The Lovers*, caused her to wonder how much importance there was to the relationship she was currently involved in. We pointed out that *The Lovers* in this context might relate to a feeling that one of the colleges might mean more to her than the other. The next card, *The Devil*, suggested there was an undercurrent of considerations that came from a deeper level. The client agreed and said that her current tutor, whom she did not get on with, was trying to prompt her to accept a particular college where he had been a student. *Justice*, which followed, seemed to point to a desire to see fair play and that the outcome should not be chosen simply by a desire for opportunities to come but should rather be a more balanced decision. *The Road*, her next card, seemed to enforce her uncertainty, but *The Moon*, following on from this, suggested that her emotions were dictating her choice and could be better employed helping her to move on. The last two cards in the spiral, *The Teacher* and *Tradition*, lifted the reading into another level. *The Teacher* clearly indicated herself, since it was her long-term goal to undertake such a role, while *Tradition* perfectly fitted the direction of her studies, which focussed on traditional lore and ancient texts. She was deeply satisfied with this, since the college offering her the best options was also famed for its work in these areas. Although she had not asked to be advised which college to choose, the whole reading had exactly outlined her situation and showed her that there was really only one choice. She opted to go ahead with the prestigious seat of learning, and we heard later that she was more than happy with her decision and the accuracy of the reading.

...

With these examples we hope to have shown you the best way to work with *The Fool's New Journey Tarot*. Armed with this deck and a desire to explore every aspect of The Fool's pathways, both old and new, we hope you find your own journey strengthened and supported through the use of the cards we have devised.

ACKNOWLEDGMENTS

To Caitlín, as ever, for her tireless help and support, and for allowing us to use some of her ideas about readings outlined in *The Time Changer's Tarot;* to Charles, for his amazing visualizations of *The Fool's New Journey,* and to Dwina and Severine, for their enthusiasm for this breakout project. Thank you also to Andre Aste for his generous and insightful foreword.

—JM

FURTHER READING AND RESOURCES

There are more new books about Tarot every year to even begin to list them all here. These are a handful of those that were most influential in the working out of *The Fool's New Journey Tarot*.

Gray, Eden. *The Complete Guide to the Tarot*. New York: Bantam Doubleday Dell, 1982.

Matthews, Caitlín. *Untold Tarot*. Atglen, PA: REDFeather, 2018.

Matthews, Caitlín. *The Time Changer's Tarot*. Atglen, PA: RED-Feather, 2024.

Pollack, Rachel. *78 Degrees of Wisdom*. Newburyport, MA: Weiser, 2018.

Pollack, Rachel. *Tarot Wisdom: Spiritual Teachings and Deeper Meanings*. Woodbury, MN: Llewellyn, 2008.

For information about titles from John and Caitlín Matthews, along with workshops and training courses, please visit our website at www.//hallowquest.org.uk

ABOUT THE AUTHORS

John Matthews is a folklorist, historian, and Tarot creator. His best-known works are *Pirates* (Carlton/Athenaeum), a *New York Times Review* bestseller for 22 weeks, and *The Winter Solstice*, which won the Benjamin Franklin Award. His book *Arthur of Albion* won a Gold Medal from NAPPA, a gold Moonbeams award, and a BIB Golden Apple Award. *The Wildwood Tarot*, coauthored with Mark Ryan, has sold over half a million copies worldwide and is the second-bestselling Tarot of all time. John has been involved in several media projects as an advisor and contributor. He was the historical advisor to the Jerry Bruckheimer movie *King Arthur* and has made numerous appearances on both the History Channel and the Discovery Channel specials. In 2021 he appeared in all eight episodes the Discovery+ series *Nostradamus: End of Days*. He shared a BAFTA award for his work on the educational DVD made to accompany the *King Arthur* movie. His most recent work includes *The Tarot of Light and Shadow* (with Andrea Aste), *The Beowulf Oracle* (with Joe Machine), and *The Goblin Market Tarot* (with Charles Newington).

Charles Newington is a UK artist whose work has been shown and published worldwide. Specializing in etching, he works with many well-known contemporary artists. His career has taken him down many different paths that include founding Alecto Historical Editions, restoring and printing for the Tate Gallery and the Society of Antiquaries, creating artwork for rock bands (including Led Zeppelin), and much more. Illustrator of *The Goblin Market Tarot*, Charles is exhibited internationally.